Operation Bangladesh

Operation Bangladesh

Colonel P. K. Gautam (Retd.)

Manas Publications
New Delhi-110002 (INDIA)

Manas Publications
(Publishers, Distributors, Importers & Exporters)
4858, Prahlad Street,
24, Ansari Road, Darya Ganj,
New Delhi - 110 002 (INDIA)
Ph.: 23260783, 23265523:, 23842660 (R)
Fax: 011-23272766
E-mail: manaspublications@vsnl.com

2007

ISBN 81-7049-273-4
Rs. 495/-

Typeset at
Manas Publications

Printed in India at
Salasar Imaging Process, Delhi
and Published by Mrs Suman Lata for
Manas Publications, 4858, Prahlad Street,
24, Ansari Road, Darya Ganj,
New Delhi - 110 002 (INDIA)

Contents

List of Maps & Sketches 7

List of Photographs 8

Acknowledgements 9

Foreword 11

Preface 13

1. On Joining 27 (Poonch) Medium Battery 15

2. The Big Picture 27

3. Opening Rounds 37

4. The Battles of Belonia Bulge 49

5. The December 1971 War 69

Appendices:

Appendix A — A Brief History of 24 Mountain Regiment 87

Annexure to Appendix A—"The Unclaimed Honour Title of 12 Poonch Mountain Battery" and Corresspondence 97

Appendix B — Characteristics of 5.5 Inch Gun 123

Appendix C — Selected All Ranks 131

Appendix D — Details of Artillery Equipment 137

Appendix E — Gunnery Problems Encountered 139

Appendix F — Sportsmanship and War 143

Annotated Bibliography 145

Annexure to Bibliography 171

Index 181

List of Maps & Sketches

Map 1 Map of Bangladesh 30

Map 2 57 & 23 Mountain Division Sectors 44

Map 3 Belonia Salient 50

Map 4 Broad Deployment in Belonia Salient: Operation Harvest 59

Map 5 Advance to Chandpur 72

Map 6 The Medium Gun Area: Advance Upto Chandpur 74

Sketch 1 The Problem of Advancing into the Line of Fire at Belonia (Plan View) 60

Sketch 2 Open Action near Hajiganj at noon on December 8, 1997 (Plan View) 27 (Poonch) Medium Battery 80

Sketch Map of Belonia Bulge 179

List of Photographs

Photograph 1	5.5 Inch Gun in Action	127
Photograph 2	Kraz 214 B	128
Photographs 3 and 4	Jat Sikh Medium Gunner	129

Acknowledgements

This book, written in parts, during the autumn and winter of 1996-97, and thereafter updated and improved, till the year 2006, would not have been possible without the vast treasure of books and other such material which was available in the United Service Institution of India, and its most helpful and cheerful library staff. I thank Dr. Sudha Raman, Research Coordinator at the United Service Institution of India, who suggested the idea of this book, edited and corrected my initial and final drafts and gave valuable suggestions. Squadron Leader RTS Chhina (Retd), of the USI Centre of Armed Forces Historical Research, also gave me many good suggestions. The response of Commanding Officers of 24 Medium Regiment (Self Propelled), 57 and 198 Mountain Regiments, 1831 Light Regiment, Commander of 23 Artillery Brigade, and Commanding Officers of 2 RAJPUT and 9 KUMAON, helped me in cross-checking dates and events for greater accuracy. I also want to thank Lieutenant Colonel VK Gupta (then a Lieutenant, the Gun Position Officer of Romeo/243 Medium Battery of 24 Medium Regiment), and Lieutenant Colonel MC Ramanand, the Battery Commander of 27 (Poonch) Medium Battery, during the war, and Lieutenant Colonels NS Rana and Swarajinder Singh who answered almost all my queries and helped me update my memories; the last two being course-mates and fellow Gun Position Officers, in 59 and 23 Mountain Regiments. I also thank Lieutenant Colonel VK Kalia and Lieutenant Colonel VS Walia who were Observation Post and Gun Position Officers in

57 and 197 Mountain Regiments, for their help in refreshing my memory. I am grateful, in particular, to Lieutenant General Ashish Banerjee, PVSM (Retd.), who was our Commanding Officer, for the Foreword. My acknowledgements to Havaldar VP Tambare, who painstakingly typed the manuscript on a 286 Personal Computer, and to Subedar P Natarajan, for creating tables and maps and formatting the final draft. Later, the maps were scanned by Shri Yashpal Bisht, at the USI, and Mrs Aparna Roy, and 'they also helped in recovering my lost electronic data, by scanning many pages. Many thanks to all of them. I thank Lt. Col. R McCaig, MC for his correspondence and sending me a letter written to him by Maj. GNF Elsworth TD. These letters allowed me to include a unique set of historical records of the Burma Campaign, World War II.

With hindsight, I can now proudly thank my mother (Amma) and sisters (Peenu, Kisho and Phuli) and the postal address system of the Army (c/o 99 Army Post Office), which led them to believe that. I was not in the war—as they had seen me off to join my regiment, in North East Frontier Agency, on the Chinese border—and could never imagine that we would pull out from the hills to take active part in the war. As a result, I never got anxious letters and finicky inquiries about my whereabouts and safety, and could devote all my energies to my job of soldiering.

Finally I thank my late wife Ashu and my daughter Nandita for bearing with my research and writing and for providing an ambience and comfort of a family.

P K Gautam

Foreword

For the medium gunners of 24 Medium Regiment, the Bangladesh War brought out learning opportunities in two distinct aspects of handling of artillery in battle.

The first, concerned the rapid movement of the regiment-less battery, from its permanent location in the Tenga Valley, Arunachal Pradesh, to concentration areas, near the eastern borders of (then) East-Pakistan. This move was a long one, over roads that ranged in quality, from good to fairly poor, and involved negotiating a number of weak/suspect bridges, by the medium guns. Diversions on the spot had to be made by the men, wherever the bridges seemed particularly weak, in order to get the guns through to battle locations, as quickly as possible. Fired up with enthusiasm that comes from anticipation of going to war, the men took these challenges in their stride and the gun columns arrived in the concentration areas, in excellent shape.

The real problems of movement of the medium guns, however, were to be encountered inside Bangladesh after the offensive was launched on a broad front. The speed of advance called for the rapid movement of the medium guns, over roads and tracks that were often in dreadfully poor condition, and dilapidated bridges and culverts which the guns had necessarily to detour. In such situations which were a daily feature during the short war, we saw tremendous cooperation between the Sappers and the gun crews. Their combined effort provided the required mobility to the medium guns, which in turn, enabled the assaulting formations to maintain the momentum of advance. More than one enemy commander, subsequently during the surrender ceremony at Maynamati, acknowledged to me, the devastating effect the medium guns had, on the morale of the Pakistani troops.

The other aspect of employment of artillery, that comes through time and again, was that, let alone the regiment, even the batteries rarely had an opportunity to deploy concentrated, as such. Before the start of the main offensive, the third battery also came down from its Sela defences, to join the regiment, in support of 4 Corps, and was allotted to 8 Mountain Division. The medium gun, due to its much longer range and its much heavier shell, compared to that of the other available guns, was in constant demand by the supported troops over the entire corps front. This often left no other option but to distribute the guns in sections to columns, for specific tasks/durations and then revert to their batteries thereafter. During those two weeks, it was a continuous sequence of deployment, move and redeployment for the medium guns to ensure that the leading troops were never held back, for want of fire support. In this mission, 24 Medium Regiment was completely successful, thanks to those great gunners.

Col. PK Gautam was a brand new young officer when all this happened. He, in fact, got fully involved with the move and concentration of the regiment, right from day one. Thereafter, he saw the battle from the gun-end, as well as FOO, with the assaulting troops. That was an enriching experience for a newly commissioned officer. It speaks volumes of his sense of history and enthusiasm, that he has come out with an account of the Bangladesh War, as he experienced it. That is really the scope of his book, and in the treatment of the subject, he is accurate and charitable. This is the story of a Medium Regiment which had a job to do in war and which it did well.

Lt. Gen. Ashish Banerjee, PVSM (Retd.)

Preface

One's first experience of a major event always leaves deep and lasting impressions. Those of us, commissioned into the army in 1970/71, were witness and participants, as subalterns, in the famous and historic liberation of Bangladesh. In the East, it was a battle of manoeuvre and movement, which is the key to winning a decisive campaign in modern war. The generalship and political leadership from the strategic angle have been well documented, and so have the histories of most of the units which participated. But the battle accounts and experiences of the creator of the maxim and lethal fire-power-that is the sole medium artillery unit, has not been recorded. This is one attempt at that.

In this age of continuing low intensity and limited warfare, as witnessed at Kargil in 1999, a general war, like the 1965 and 1971 Indo-Pakistani encounters, seems unlikely. Nevertheless, even in the age of information and cyber war, certain experiences, events and impressions, recorded in the memories of a raw subaltern, may still have relevance, when it comes to the practicality of fighting a major war - so fashionably termed warfighting now. The preparation of an army for a general war is a necessity for deterrence. War may be thrust upon a nation and like an insurance policy, combat readiness needs to be undertaken.

This book may be useful for the study of human nature in war as equipment, organisation and techniques may improve, but the human factor would remain the same. It also records, what was the Indian Army, during that period and era. It could be an actual "Subaltern Study", from the point of view of professional historians, that is, history not from the pen of a General, but from that of a subaltern. These have been possible due to academic hindsight and the books now available on the war. Barring occasional use of a radio transistor, I do not recall having access to journals and newspapers during the operations. TV coverage was yet to be commercialised and probably only some areas of the capital had some black and white TV coverage. The inclination to study newspapers and magazines was not there, nor were any available. It was more important to master one's skills and be with the men, to know and work with them. There was no media coverage of our sector with the forward troops, and we never met any Indian or foreign war correspondent, though it is learnt that some did operate in selected areas, in the rear or in other sectors, including women reporters from European and Western countries. This" privacy" in war, what we experienced, is not possible now, due to the media wars of the present age. During 1971, STD was unheard of and one had to spend days in getting through via trunkdialing, provided you were near a proper communication centre of a corps or division HQ, which, probably only the personnel from the Corps of Signals had access to, besides senior commanders. With the present age of ISD, STD, mobiles, electronic media and the internet, where one keeps ringing up or contacting people in real time or its reverse—uninterrupted soldiering is surely history.

This account is also a continuum of the history of 27 (Poonch) Mountain Battery, which was the erstwhile 12 (Poonch) Mountain Battery during the world wars. This book is also a tribute to the finest of the soldiers—the Jat Sikhs, sturdiest of the medium guns (5.5 inch of UK), and the most rugged and gunner-friendly Field Artillery Tractor Kraz 214B (erstwhile USSR).

P K Gautam

1

On Joining 27 (Poonch) Medium Battery

"You have been posted to 24 Medium Regiment[1]—tough troops, tough area", were the words of Colonel SK Talwar,[2] Chief Instructor, Field Wing, at the School of Artillery, Devlali, in May 1971. On checking out with colleagues, I came to know that the tough troops were Jat Sikhs and the tough area was the area of operations of 5 Mountain Division, to include Sela and Bomdila, in North East Frontier Agency or NEFA (now renamed as Arunachal Pradesh). Our special leg training on the equipment, with which our units were equipped, then commenced. We were quite impressed with the 5.5 inch medium gun,3 which was a much heavier and bigger piece, than the 25 pounder gun, on which all the young officers had been trained initially. It had seen service in Burma, during the Second World War.

Newly commissioned officers from the Indian Military Academy (IMA) at Dehradun, used to head straight to the School of Artillery, Devlali, in Maharashtra, for the initial introduction to gunnery. The training period was for about five months. After a common syllabus, based on the basic gun, the 25 pounder—and towards the end of the course, we were allotted our units. One could opt for mountain regiments, a number of which had mules artillery for draught power, and also for the various tactical loads, or the field regiments, which were integral to the Infantry divisions, and like the mountain regiments, were integrated with the infantry for battle. Medium regiments were considered sophisticated and were then used for fire support to the armoured formations or for general support and reinforcing tasks. Ultimately, it was the Military Secretary at the Army Headquarters, who decided the postings. I was one of the five young officers, who got posted to a medium regiment, with the vintage British 5.5 inch gun, with a standard shell weight of 80 pounds. The other medium regiments had the longer range 130 mm guns from Russia. Medium Regiments equipped with 130 mm guns were the natural choice for service in the plains and deserts, which we had in plenty. Because of its capability to fire like a howitzer in high angle, the 5.5 inch gun was wisely allotted to the mountains, as its shell could be lobbed over peaks and hills, on the reverse slopes, which was not possible with the 130 mm medium gun. So, there it was. A medium unit in the mountains.

After the postings were announced, the students were divided according to the equipment they got posted to. This was the significance of this part of training, and the name tag 'special leg'. We were quite impressed with the 5.5 inch medium gun, which was a much heavier piece than the 25 pounder field gun, on which all young officers had been trained initially. It had seen service in Burma during the Second World War. Besides 24 Medium Regiments, the other 5.5 inch regiments were the 34 (Marathas), 38 (Rajputs), 39 (Sikhs), and 40 (South Indians) Medium Regiments. My friend 2/Lt. Navneet Swaraj, was posted to 39 Medium Regiment*. These were very old units, with rich institutional traditions. What was exciting was that they had one class compositions. Having been allotted our units, we began the search for our unit officers and men at the School of Artillery. In the new "Bravo" Mess that day, I met two great ex-officers of my would-be regiment—Captain Paul, the national and service squash champion, and Major Athlye, who was later transferred to the Army Education Corps (AEC). The first question they asked me was, whether I was a good sportsman. Fortunately, I was a fourth string hockey player and was frank enough to tell them that though not outstanding, I will make all efforts to make it to the unit team. I understood that, to command the

---

* After the ceasefire, he was killed due to shelling, in the western sector at Chamb.

respect of the men, one needs to improve upon tough body contact and troop games*.

By mid-June, our Young Officer's Course terminated, and all of us proceeded to join our regiments. For the first time in my life, I travelled to the East—traversing Bihar, West Bengal and Assam. After two days of journey by train, I reached the transit camp at Misamari, at the Himalayan foothills of the North East Frontier Agency (NEFA). It was a newly established Transit Camp for the officers and men, transiting down or going up the hills. The next day, at 3 AM after being accommodated in an Army Service Corps convoy of 3-ton Shaktiman truck, which had wooden benches on the sides, we reached the unit base at Dahung, after about 12 hours of journey. Travelling up the hills had its own charm and I could relate to the beautiful Himalayan countryside, to the Kumaon hills, with which I was very familiar. En-route, at a place called Sessa, we were stung by a local species of mosquito-like fly, called the 'Dim Dam' fly. Its sting, unlike the mainstream Indian mosquito, resulted in an awkward swelling and itch, though it did not lead to malaria.

During the Young Officer's Course, we had heard that a newly posted young subaltern was baptised with a great deal of ragging, on joining the units. Officers would be in disguise as orderlies and drivers to receive the new entrant and disclose the truth later, and then keep the young lad on his toes, and on probation for a sufficient period of time. Unknown to me, the unit had moved further up to high altitudes, and Dahung would only have a skeleton staff, without any officers. I missed out on this probation experience. The regiment had moved up to the Sela heights, on the summer operational alert (termed 'Oopee Alert' by troops), an annual ritual to occupy the main defensive positions, during the campaigning season, at the vital ground of

* After the war, I did manage to represent the unit hockey team as a right half which did not require much skills except horse-like stamina, in defence, to neutralise the opponents left out, and in attack, feed the forwards. At times, the opportunity arose to join the leading echelons in attack. As a rule, side pushes was also my job. This involved running wildly up and down. Stamina was more important than skills. And stamina I had enough, after a commando course.

Sela, scene of the heroic and controversial battle of 1962, with the Chinese. This exercise kept everybody in trim, just in case the Chinese planned a repeat of the 1962 war.

Elements of 27 (Poonch) Medium battery had stayed back at the base, as it was rumoured that this battery was likely to move out from NEFA (or deinduct) and go to the East Pakistan border, soon. Instead of being ragged and bullied by the senior subaltern, I thus found that, I was the lone officer (and of course the base officer commanding the unit-base).

Subedar (Sub) (Driver Special Vehicle) Fakir Singh, the Senior Junior Commissioned Officer, and Naib Subedar (N/Sub) (Operator Radio Artillery) Hardip Singh of the 27(Poonch) Medium battery, greeted me and lined up the Non-Commissioned Officers (NCOs) for my introduction. It was a great experience, shaking hands and reviewing the tall and burly Jat Sikhs (average height—5 feet, 10 inches), men of my new home, my own weight not exceeding 52-53 kilograms, of medium stature.

Within a couple of days of my stay at Dahung, I received instructions to come up to Sela. I was issued with the new, indigenously manufactured, Extreme Cold Climate (ECC) clothing, comprising a coat parka and woollen serge trousers. The most fashionable part was to shed the beret or jungle cap and don the woollen balaclava, folded neatly like a 'Gandhi Cap'. Clad in my new attire, I commenced my journey, to join up with the unit. The journey took me across the famous town of Bomdila and the pass (about 9000 feet, plus), which was the depth position to repulse the Chinese, during the 1962 war. Later in life, after having read the books on our defeat at the hands of the Chinese, in 1962, I came to know that Bomdila was considered by many tacticians, as a better vital ground than the massive Sela heights ahead. Bomdila, it was mentioned, had depth, it dominated the road axis and could not be easily bypassed or outflanked. But at that time, I did not have the eye for the ground and I journeyed more as an excited military tourist, exploring a virgin land.

After Bomdila, it was a descent into a valley with interesting names, like Dirang and Sapper camp. In these areas, as go the stories of the Sino-Indian War of 1962, the cohesion of headquarters 4 Infantry Division was broken by the Chinese by surprise and outflanking moves, resulting in the infamous 'retreat of our forces', without giving an organised fight. After the valley, the road began to climb, and now, one could feel that the massive feature of Sela was nearing. In the evening, I reached the operational location of the unit, in deep and well dug out bunkers, at a location identified by the distance as 'Kilometer 97'. As it was high altitude (over 10,000 feet), one was supposed to take it easy, both mentally and physically, and get acclimatised (as usual the troops called it "climate change"), to the low level of oxygen. That night, I was not disturbed, and slept in peace.

The next morning, I reported to the unit Adjutant, Captain BCS Jagati. Evidently, most of the affiliated parties of the command and observations groups had gone out for some exercise, with the infantry. The Adjutant then made me fill my arrival details and introduced to me the environment. Then came the order that I was now to go back to Dahung, to undertake a reconnaissance of the road conditions, for move of the massive medium guns, across the plains of Assam to the state of Tripura, via Meghalaya. Having thus reported to the unit, and having filled my details, I headed back to Dahung.

Thus, within the first week of my reporting to the unit, I had the opportunity of visiting the operational location, where instead of acclimatising to the high altitudes, I was ordered to take a Jonga vehicle, with Naib Subedar (Operator) Balbir Singh, also popularly known as 'Hammer,'[4] to drive down to Shillong, in Meghalaya state, and carry out reconnaissance of the road conditions, road bends and the bridges, keeping in mind the weight, dimensions and turning circle of a 5.5 inch medium gun in tow behind a Kraz Field Artillery Tractor. The movement involved a downhill drive back to the rail head at Misamari, then cutting across the plains of Assam, via Gauhati (now called Guwahati), then onto the hilly Meghalaya state, with its famous and beautiful capital—the hill station of Shillong, with a total distance of about 400 kilometres.

Just one day before leaving for my task at Dahung, I met my Battery Commander (BC), Major CP Khopkar, and battery Second-in-Command, Captain AR Pedgaonkar, who had also come down for the impending move of the battery. I was given two pieces of valuable advice by my BC, the first that, I must know the names and characteristics of each gunner in the battery soon, and the second was that, I must look after my batman.[5] For the first advice, I bought a crib book (sort of a diary-cum-register) from the unit 'bania', and wrote down all the 120 odd names. Each of them ended with 'Singh'. There were two Havaldar Mohinder Singhs, who had to be identified with the last two digits of their army numbers, that is, Mohinder Singh-70 and Mohinder Singh-90, respectively.

Move out of NEFA

With these opening encounters and experiences of regimental life, I soon found myself commanding a Jonga vehicle, and thus commenced my military career, 'independently'. We packed our bags and set off on the downhill journey—back to the beautiful plains of Assam. Each hairpin and U-bend on the road, was measured and recorded, to establish whether the medium gun would negotiate it or not. Weak bridges and culverts were also inspected. Unlike the sappers, there were no formulae to work out the strength of a bridge. Practical commonsense and judgment was used and each bridge and culvert was declared 'fit' or 'unfit', as we journeyed down the intended route which the guns would later take*.

Till the end of June and early July, 1971, we continued independent reconnaissance of the roads and bridges. We attached ourselves to any army unit for petrol, food, boarding and lodging. Many times we cooked our own meals, or lived on fruits, and survival rations, which were very nutritious. Pineapples were ten paise a piece. During this period, I discovered that Balbir Singh was a charismatic personality. Each time we halted, dozens of children of the local villages nearby, would rush to admire, with awe, this giant of a man. Children, in any case, love to see any army column, on the move. They always peeped inside and admired the 'toys' that we carried, like water bottles, thermos flasks, binoculars, beddings, maps with pencils, etc.

---

* Later, the guns actually negotiated the weak and suspect bridges and turns and reached Tripura without much problem.

Our 'recce' was an on-job-learning process, on the need to study roads, bridges and communications. This had to be checked and plotted on the map, so that, it could be related to, later on. The capability to relate to the time and distance travelled, combined with the directions, is one great art, which one needs to have, as a second nature. I thoroughly enjoyed this experience. I was delighted to use the prismatic compass, it always gave us clues on the right directions. The 'recce' was also a lesson on good driving and maintenance of the vehicles. Like car rallyists, the driver always kept the right spares and tools.

During the course of the 'recce', I learnt a great deal about the regimental level of sports, from my party. The unit had served last, in a peace station at Clement Town in Dehradun. In peace stations, those days, only performance in sports mattered. 24 Medium Regiment had a great sporting tradition and had fought tooth and nail to win the sports championship, each year. Balbir narrated a story, which had become sort of a legend. In Dehradun, we had a tough competition from 10 Field Regiment (which had a Sikh battery) in hockey. Each match at the famous Garrison Hockey Field, near the 'Kala Ground' or the Drill Square, between the two units, resulted in some sort of violent play. In order to avoid such occurrences, there was a legend that, the General Officer Commanding, whose Flag Staff House was within earshot distance to the hockey field, could not bear it any more, and himself referred the match. On a previous occasion, the Commander Artillery had to intervene, and show the 'red' and 'yellow' cards to the ferocious players.‡ These stories were interludes and the only

‡ This clash of units, while playing hockey at the Kala Ground area, had a cyclic and a legendary life. In the mid-1980s, while serving in a newly raised 143 Field Regiment, during a match between two Sikh artillery units (53 Field and 193 Field Regiments), the ritual was repeated, and all the officer spectators had to enter the hockey ground, to stop the violent fights that had erupted between the two teams, and also the spectators. Another legendary hockey clash was the famous incidence of 4 GRENADIERS and 9 PUNJAB at Ambala in early 1960s. I thank the retired senior community at NOIDA in giving me this information.

entertainment for us, by recalling the good old sporting days of peace-time soldiering.

Having reached Shillong, in early July, while attached with 183 Light Regiment, we got a message to report back at Misamari, at the foothills of the Himalayas. Misamari, was the rail-head, from where all train movement of units, coming down from the hills or going up, would begin or end. The news was that, the battery had moved out of NEFA and was to go by road, towards the border with East Pakistan. Instead of going by road with the guns, I was to command a special train, conveying ammunition from Misamari to Badarpur, on the only metre gauge railway track. The guns would move by road, under arrangement of the battery Commander. I reached Misamari and submitted the 'recce' report, and joined up with the train party. At the railway siding, I found that the gunners were shunting and pushing the covered wagons manually, to facilitate the loading of ammunition from ramps or straight from the trucks. The initiative and innovation of the train loading party, indicated a lot of practical experience, which the troops had. I found it better to be an observer, and learn just by watching my men. I was educated by the senior Non-Commissioned Officers that, it's not a must for an engine (or 'power') to be available for such tasks. Horsepower can be derived from man-power. A train move is pure logistics and one needs to master the tricks of successful loading, shunting, movement and unloading. Later in my career, while preparing for promotion examinations, I came across the memoirs of the German General Rommel, who had learnt the intricacies of logistics by coordinating train loading and shunting of trains as a junior officer.

We had a total of five to six bogies of covered wagons and common second class compartment, which we all shared. These sets of rolling stock later got attached to a train of 82 Light Regiment, under the command of Major PD Kitkule (who was later awarded the *Vir Chakra).* We were 20 to 30 personnel from the Medium battery, in a third-class compartment, to ourselves. We had our own cook house, called *Langar,* in a covered wagon. En-route, after having crossed Lumding Station, our next halt was Silchar, where we were treated to a sumptuous meal, laid out at the railway station by 23 Mountain Regiment, which comprised the famous 74 (Gwalior), 75 (Patiala) and 76 (J&K) Mountain Batteries, which till 1951, were State Forces and were taken over by the Indian Army, from April 1, 1951. The only odd thing was that, the military special had got delayed and it was 3 in the morning. Camaraderie and *espirit-de-corps* was more intoxicating than any rum, and Subedar Wariam Singh from 23 Mountain Regiment was our gracious host.

We reached our destination, Badarpur in about five days of travelling time by train. By this time, the road column with the guns had already reached Badarpur, and had set up a tented camp. In the final stretch of the road journey, the guns were ferried across on rafts, prepared by the divisional engineers, as the bridge was too narrow and weak to bear the load of the guns in tow, behind the Kraz vehicle. At Badarpur the battery got together again. Now began a new phase of my regimental life, that was training with the troops.

As was the regimental practice, I was trained, and made to perform the tasks of a gunner and a No. 1 (Detachment Commander) of a gun. I was put under command of Charlie 2 (C2) gun of Havaldar Mohinder Singh-90 and his gun, second-in-command, Naik Darshan Singh, who made me do the gun drill with the detachment. Subedar Faqir Singh trained me to drive the Kraz 214B, which had an unpowered steering, and one had to literally wrestle with the wheel and steering. I became a part of the gun detachment and enjoyed the training thoroughly. I found that, I was living up to the expectations of my men.

In the fourth week of July 1971, the battery moved out of the camp location at Badarpur, and occupied a gun area, next to the border. This was my first experience of moving in a tactical fashion, on a road. After deployment of the guns, the training resumed. The more one practices, the better one becomes, with the technical aspects and also the equipment. I continued to perform all the duties of a gun detachment, exactly the way the gunners would have done. Fortunately, our training at the School of Artillery had been thorough, and I passed all tests, set by my instructors. I could prove my worth by performing all the technical duties to the satisfaction of my senior JCO. He must have declared me fit, as, on July 28, I was elevated up by the battery Commander to perform the duties of a Gun Position Officer (GPO), which happened to be my official appointment.

On that day of July 28, 1971, we continued with our command post exercise with guns, unaware that soon, the first rounds, as they say, would be fired in "anger". But before resuming the story, something about the over-all situation, leading to 27(Poonch} Medium battery having been deployed in action for the first time, after the 1965 War, must be told. This is covered in the next chapter.

End Notes

1. For a brief History of the 24 Medium Regiment, till the 1965 Indo-Pakistan War, readers may refer to Appendix A. An overview of some major actions by 27 (Poonch) Medium battery [then called 12 (Poonch) Mountain battery], during the Second World War, in the Burma Campaign, have been covered in the *Artillery Journal,* 1988, published by Regiment of Artillery Association in an article entitled, 'The Unsung Valour of Mountain battery', by the author. The article is reproduced, as Annexure to Appendix A The *Royal Artillery Journal,* from UK, in its September 1996 issue (Volume CXXIII No. 2), featured articles by participants in Burma. One such response, as a letter to the Editor, which was published with replies from the author of the article, Lieutenant Colonel R McCiag, MC, and a letter is also included in the Annexure to Appendix A. For further details of the operations of 12 (Poonch) Mountain battery, during World War II, readers are advised to read *The History of Indian Mountain Artillery,* by Brigadier General C.A.L. Graham (Aldershot : Gale and Polden Limited, 1957). For a first-hand account of life in a mountain battery, during the Second World War, an article entitled '12 (Poonch) Indian Mountain battery in World War II',

by the then battery Commander, Major A.B. Howard, in *Tales of the Mountain Gunners,* Edited by C.H.T. MacFetridge and J.P. Warsen (William Blackwood, Edinburg 1973), may be referred.

2. Colonel S.K. Talwar later retired as a Major General. He was also the Commandant of the School of Artillery, Devlali, in 1980s.

3. For a brief technical characteristic of 5.5 inch gun, readers may consult Appendix B.

4. Balbir Singh had been a national hammer throw champion, and as I was told, he was beaten by the famous Pravin Kumar (of Border Security Force, and later, an actor, who performed as 'Bhim', in the television serial *Mahabharat,* as the story went later) in the event. Throughout his Army career, Balbir Singh had mostly been training and practising for athletics, as was the norm, and at the same time, he was exceptionally outstanding in his duties as a Gunner.

5. The term 'Batman', or Orderly, has now been replaced with *Sahayak,* who is generally a radio operator, during operations. I had the honour of having Operator Radio Artillery, Sher Singh, as my *Sahayak,* who was with me throughout the operations. The second advice of my battery Commander was, "Look after your Batman", was heeded in a different fashion. It was he (Sher Singh), who looked after my frugal personal needs of wartime administration, and allowed me to concentrate all my energies to my basic 'kingpin' job of a Gun Position Officer. The names of persons whom I can now recall during the operations have been summarised at Appendix C.

2

The Big Picture

Political Situation

The division or partition of India and Pakistan, on August 15, 1947, was based on the two-nation theory. Muslim-dominated areas in the western and eastern flanks of India became West Pakistan, and East Pakistan. The two-nation theory was the basis of Pakistan which believed that the Muslims and the Hindus could not co-exist together, as a nation. India, on the other hand believed in a pluralistic society.

East Pakistan had a majority of Bengalis, while West Pakistan was dominated by Punjabis, Pathans, Sindhis, the Mujahirs or the refugees from mostly, Uttar Pradesh (UP), from the Indo- Gangetic plains and adjoining regions. After the creation of East and West Pakistan, the economic aspirations of East Pakistan, and its expectations in the governance of Pakistan, as a whole, was not in equal proportion to the population or the natural resources. Not surprisingly, there was a drift between the Bengalis of East Pakistan and the West Pakistan. In spite of having a majority, the Bengalis were not given the political power they deserved and were entitled to. Pakistan, soon after gaining independence, had army rule, under Field Marshal Ayub Khan. Ayub Khan handed over power to General Yahya Khan in 1969. Under General Yahya Khan, Pakistan held its first general elections in October 1970. By December 1970, the results were declared. Out of the 300 seats, 162 were allocated to East-Pakistan, where the Awami League, under Mujibur Rahman won 160 seats, but not a single seat in West Pakistan. The West Pakistan dominated, Pakistan

People's Party (PPP) won 81 out of the 136 seats, in West Pakistan but not a single seat in East Pakistan. After the elections, Yahya Khan announced that, National Assembly would meet in East Pakistan, in March 1971, to frame a new constitution. Mujib put up a Six-Point Proposal. Matters could not be resolved by political means and on March 25, 1971, the Army clamped down on the Bengalis in East Pakistan. The Bengali units and personnel were eliminated. West Pakistani soldiers, stationed in East Pakistan, became an occupation-force.

Thus started the Bengali insurgency, and struggle for freedom in East-Pakistan. As the insurgency picked up momentum, the refugees influx to India became unbearable. India, gradually provided diplomatic, and political support for the freedom movement in Bangladesh. Indian military had to intervene, leading to the creation of Bangladesh.

The last two wars between India and Pakistan had taken place over the Jammu & Kashmir state in 1947-48, and in 1965. In these, only the Western borders had hostilities, and East Pakistan had remained dormant. Now, in 1971, the focus of conflict suddenly shifted to East Pakistan. A general and a full-scale war over East Pakistan must have been a low probability or contingency for the planners. It was during this period, probably in the month of April, that the Chief of the Army Staff (COAS), General SHFJ Manekshaw, advised the political leadership to conduct the operations, in the winter of 1971, as that was the ideal time to campaign, rather than rushing headlong immediately, in April or May, without proper mobilisation and logistics preparation. Winter also was the time, that the Chinese would not be able to launch a worthwhile offensive, as the Himalayan passes would be covered and clogged with snow.

Terrain

Bangladesh consists of alluvial plains, formed by the deposits of three mighty rivers, the Ganga, and the Brahmaputra (called Jamuna in Bangladesh) which combine North-West of Dacca with the Ganga, to become Padma, the Meghna river confluences with Padma south of Dacca. These mighty rivers, even in the dry winter season, from November to April, are so wide, that it appears that one is standing on a sea beach. The countryside is criss-crossed with numerous tributaries and nullahs. The soil is a mixture of clay, silt and sand. The groundwater level is very high. The region's transport and communication have been influenced by the rivers. Local populace depends mostly on boats and ferries. The railways and roads, roughly conform to the flow of major rivers, in the north-south direction. (See Map 1)

Military Situation

Militarily, the operations can be divided into four phases, as under[1]:

(a) **Phase 1:** From March 25,1971, till June 1971, when there was a spontaneous and uncoordinated resistance to the Pakistan Army in East Pakistan, by rebels and freedom fighters. It was during this stage that the Chief of the Army Staff, General SHFJ Manekshaw, clearly explained and convinced the political leadership that, an immediate response was ruled out, and the Army needed time for logistics preparations, and also had to wait for the campaigning season, during the winter months, when a large-scale movement would be possible, in the terrain of East Pakistan and the Chinese threat would be the least, on account of snowfall on the Himalayan passes.

(b) **Phase 2:** From July to October 1971, the *Mukti Fauj* organised themselves, as *Mukti Bahini* and carried out training and small-scale retaliatory raids, assisted by artillery support.

(c) **Phase 3:** November 1971 to December 3, 1971, when guerrilla operations were stepped up; there was extensive use of artillery and tanks and as a preliminary operation, the Indian Army, with elements of reorganised *Mukti Bahini,* launched simultaneous limited operation on key-border regions, in retaliation. The logistics and mobilisation preparations were also completed during this period, and various contingencies had been worked out by the Indian Armed Forces. Air Force on both sides, also commenced participation during this phase.

(d) **Phase 4:** 3 December to December 16, 1971. An all-out war on both Western and Eastern fronts, culminating in the 'liberation of Bangladesh'.

MAP NOT TO SCALE

At the command level, the area of operations of IV Corps was in the Eastern Sector, bounded by River Meghna in the west, Meghalaya in the north, Tripura and Mizo Hills in the east and Bay of Bengal in the south. 8 Mountain Division, earmarked for counter-insurgency operations in North-East India, was opposite Sylhet. 57 Mountain Division, located at North Tripura, at Agartala, was opposite Akhaura, Brahmanbaria, and Ashuganj Sectors. Further south, 23 Mountain Division was opposite Comilla and Maynamati; the two important border cantonments. In addition, the Corps was allotted Kilo Force consisting of two infantry battalions, supported by four battalions worth of *Mukti Bahini* and Border Security Force, with artillery.

The Corps Maintenance Area (CMA) was developed at Teliamura, using a single metre gauge rail axis through Assam till Dharmanagar, and thereafter logistics preparations continued on class 9 (class 9 means, a road including bridges, just fit enough to take the traffic of 3 ton trucks), one-way roads and tracks, down to Agartala in the south, a distance of 200 kilometres and beyond, to the tip of Tripura. Logistically, it could be appreciated, a major thrust from this sector appeared unlikely. However, it is now certain that our generals[2] who planned and executed the operations, had undoubtedly done the most extraordinary movement of operational art and could be compared to the German thrust through Ardeness, during World War II, which under similar mindsets had forced most of the enemy commanders to conclude that a thrust, logistically, was unlikely.[3]

Where Did the Medium Gunners Fit In ?

In this broad picture, the grouping and attachments of the only medium regiment in IV Corps Zone, is easy to understand. Generally, one battery was to support each of the division. In November 1971, 26 (Murree) Medium battery, with five guns (as against the authorised six) of the regiment, moved down from NEFA, leaving a lone gun, to take on any Chinese thrust. This battery supported operations of 8 Mountain Division from the first week of December 1971; Regimental Headquarters and 27 (Poonch) Medium battery came under 23 Mountain Division, from middle of October till ceasefire, and 243 Medium battery which was in support of 57 Mountain Division till November split into two troops of three guns each; the left troop moved north and supported 8 Mountain Division from November 21 to December 4, 1971, till relieved by 26 (Murree) Medium battery, and joined the right troop by December 5/6, 1971. The right troop earlier during, mid-November 1971 had moved to be a part of 23 Mountain Division, 28 Medium battery of 40 Medium Regiment, replaced 243 Medium battery, in support of 57 Mountain Division, from November 8/9, 1971. By first week of December, the medium batteries were in support, as under:

(a) 8 Mountain Division— 26 (Murree) Medium battery of five guns, under Major GM Lasrado as Battery Commander. Captain Satish Chand Diwan, as Observation Post Officer and Second Lieutenant Kartar Singh, as Gun Position Onicer Subedar Thaman Singh was the Senior Junior Commissioned Officer.

(b) 57 Mountain Division— 28 Medium battery of 40 Medium Regiment (South Indian Troops).

(c) 23 Mountain Division— (a) 27 (Poonch) Medium battery.

(b) 243 Medium battery under Major Jadhav as Battery Commander and Second Lieutenant VK Gupta as Gun Position Officer.

(c) Regimental Headquarters 24 Medium Regiment, under the command of Lieutenant Colonel Ashish Banerjee, with Major Iqbal Singh Loomba, as Second-in-Command, Captain BCS Jagati Adjutant, Captain

RS Rathee (son of the legendary late Brigadier Hoshiar Singh, of 1962 Sino-Indian War), Regimental Medical Officer, Captain (Selected List) DL Sharma, Quarter Master, Captains KC Sharma, SC Bajaj, PR Ranga Rao, Lieutenant JS Jodha and Capt. CD Chawla from the Electrical and Mechanical Engineers was the officer-in-charge of the Light Repair Workshop.

Deployment of Pakistan Army[4]

In the Eastern portion (opposite Indian 4 Corps) of East Pakistan, the deployment of Pakistan was as under:

(a) 14 Infantry Division : The Divisional Headquarters (Major General Qazi Abdul Majeed) was moved out from Dacca to Bhairab Bazar, in November 1971. The Division was responsible for the area from Sylhet, Maulvi Bazar, down to Saldanadi. The dispositions of its Brigades were:

(i) **27 Infantry Brigade (Brigadier Saadullah Khan) :** Brigade Headquarters at Brahmanbaria. Brigade was responsible for area from Madhupur to Saldanadi.

(ii) **202 Infantry Brigade (Brigadier Saleemullah) :** Brigade Headquarters at Sylhet. Brigade was responsible for defence of Sunamganj, Jantiapur to Sholpur.

(iii) **313 Infantry Brigade (Brigadier Iftikar Rana) :** Brigade Headquarters at Maulvi Bazar. Brigade was responsible from Latu to Titas River.

(b) 39 Infantry Division : This Division was raised in October 1971, under the command of Major General Rahim Khan and was made responsible for the defence of the area, east of River Meghna, from Saldanadi to the border with Burma.

The Divisional Headquarters was established at the river port of Chandpur, on the Meghna River. This division was pitted against 23 Mountain Division, with which 27 (Poonch) Medium battery played a dominant role, in delivery of long range firepower, its organisation:

(i) **Artillery**

(aa) 53 Field Regiment (105 mm guns)

(ab) 171 Mortar Battery

(ii) 17 Infantry Brigade: (Brigadier Atif, hockey player of Olympic fame) with Headquarters located at Comilla (see Map 2). The brigade was responsible for areas like Saldanadi, Comilla, Laksham and Daukhandi, with the following troops :

(aa) **30 PUNJAB:** Responsible from Saldanadi to Mian Bazar.

(ab) **25 Frontier Force (FF):** From Mian Bazar, Lalmaki to Daudkhandi.

(ac) **23 PUNJAB:** From Comilla to Chaudagram.

(ad) 13 guns of 53 Field Regiment provided artillery support.

(iii) **53 Infantry Brigade:** (Brigadier Aslam Khan Niazi, no relation of the famous General Niazi). Brigade Headquarters was located at Feni. The brigade was responsible for areas such as Chaudagram, Feni, and Belonia, with the following troops :

(aa) 15 BALUCH (deployed inside Belonia Bulge)

(ab) 39 BALUCH

(ac) 21 Azad Kashmir (AK) one company only

(ad) 5 guns of 53 Field Regiment provided artillery support

(iv) **91 Infantry Brigade (Brigadier Taskeen-Ud-Din):** The battalion Headquarters of 21 AK was moved to Karer Hat, to act as Brigade Headquarters, for 91 Infantry Brigade, in November 1971, after capture of Belonia Bulge by the Indian Army, to guard the Feni-Chittagong Road. 91 Adhoc Brigade was responsible for areas such as Ramgarh, Kartar Hat, Chittagong Hill Tracts, and East of River Feni, with the following troops:

(aa) Two Companies, 24 Frontier Force (FF)

(ab) East Pakistan Civil Armed Forces (EPCAF-One Wing)

(ac) Rangers—One Battalion

(ad) Mujahid—One Battalion

(ae) 171 Mortar battery less a troop

(v) **97 Infantry Brigade (Brigadier Atta Malik):** The brigade Headquarters was located at Chittagong. Brigade was responsible for Chittagong Hill Tracts to the border with Burma, with the following troops:

(aa) 48 BALUCH

(ab) 24 FF less two companies

(ac) 2 Commando (less company)

(ad) EPCAF—One Wing

(ae) Marine Battalion

(af) Troop, 171 Mortar battery

(vi) **Armour:** The number of tanks, as quoted by Pakistani authors, vary from none to two.[6]

(vii) **Air:** The Pakistan Air Force (PAF) was rendered out of action, during air operations by the Indian Air Force (IAF). Their was total supremacy of the skies, when the war broke out in December 1971.

End Notes

1. Sisson Richard and Rose E. *War & Secession* : *Pakistan, India and Creation of Bangladesh,* Vistaar Publications, New Delhi, 1990, pp. 208-215; and Islam Rafiquil, *A Tale of Millions: Bangladesh Liberation War 1971,* Anna 38/2 Bangla Bazar, Dhaka, 1974, p. 224.

2. The Generalship of the Chief of the Army Staff, General SHFJ Manekshaw, the General Officer Commanding in

Chief, Eastern Command, Lieutenant General Jagjit Singh Aurora, Major General JFR Jacob, Chief of Staff, have been well praised and recorded. See Rajendra Nath, PVSM, Major General, *Military Leadership in India: Vedic Period to Indo Pak War;* Lancers Books, 1990, Chapter 17 (Indo-Pak War, 1971). At the corps level, the tactical genius of Lieutenant General Sagat Singh, General Officer Commanding 4 Corps has been recognised. The quick breakthroughs were no doubt achieved by the bold tactics of deep penetration and enveloping moves, upsetting the Information-Decision-Action (IDA) cycle of the Pakistani commanders. It was *Auftragstaktik* par excellence.

3. Julian Thomson, op.cit., *The Lifeblood of War;* Brassey's (UK), 1991. The author has given our general logistics staff, a pride of place by placing it in a historical context between the Yom Kippur War 1973 and the Falklands Campaign of 1982, (Chapter 7, 'War in a Snipe March : Bangladesh 1971', pp. 234-245). The nuts and bolts of administrative planning and preparations are yet to be recorded. See also RB Khanna, *Sappers War;* pp. 92-93, Engineer-in-Chief Directorate, 1995. During the preparatory stage, about 30,000 tons of stores were required from Assam and areas to its west, and over 900 kilometres of roads were constructed or improved in Tripura, in seven weeks, before hostilities commenced.
4. Riza, Shaukat. Major General (Retd.), *The Pakistan Army;* 1966-71, Services Book Club, Lahore, Pakistan, 1990, Chapter VI.
5. Ibid, p.156.
6. Salik Siddiq, *Witness to Surrender;* Oxford University Press, Karachi, 1977, p.172.

3

Opening Rounds

Aatgram and Chargram

Finally we were deployed on that day of July 28, 1971, after successfully having moved out of NEFA, with our medium guns. Simultaneously, we also devoted a lot of time to training. Even in field and operational conditions, there was no let up in the probationary programme of a youngster like me. I was the Gun Position Officer that day and like business as usual, we were engrossed in our training. Our sister battery or 243 Medium battery, had followed the wake and had also landed up next to us that day. I was so busy that I did not get time to go and meet the personnel of 243 Medium battery. We then got instructions to prepare live ammunition.

A *Mukti Fauj* raid on a Pakistani border out post at Aatgram and Chargram had been planned. The observation group support was given by 23 Mountain Regiment of 57 Artillery Brigade, and Major S Jadhav of 243 Medium battery, CP Khopkar of 27(Poonch) Medium battery with Captain MC Ramanand. The freshly inducted 27(Poonch) and 243 Medium Batteries were to be used for the first time, as a retaliatory measure. Fire orders were received on radio and my Senior JCO prompted me to check 'ASLI'[1], which I did, and soon, the opening ranging rounds were fired. Both the batteries engaged about three to four targets, and by evening, the firing was called off for 27 (Poonch) Medium battery. We were informed by the observers that we had hit an ammunition dump during a precision shoot, using a single gun and the shooting was good. Having thus fired the first rounds into East Pakistan, the gunners displayed their remarkably high morale. 27 (Poonch) Medium battery then pulled back to Badarpur. The guns were ferried across the river, near Badarpur, on a class 40 raft, specially built by 15 Engineer Regiment. Later, 243 Medium battery was deployed, further North. They fired 150 rounds to support a *Mukti Fauj* attack on Latu Railway Station, Sylhet district, Pramodnagar area, with Major S Jadhav, as battery Commander-cum-Observation Post Officer, and Lieutenant JS Jodha, as Gun Position Officer .

Between August and October, the Regiment Headquarters also joined us from NEFA, and the entire Regiment, minus 26 (Murree) Medium battery had concentrated at Tripura. By then, the three Indian Corps around East Pakistan, had started concentrating, starting with the newly raised 2 Corps in the West, 33 Corps in the North-West, 101 Communication Zone in the North, and 4 Corps in the East. We were the only medium gunners, initially in the entire 4 Corps Zone, and were placed under command of 57 Mountain Division at Agartala. The broad outline of the formations and units of 57 Mountain Division is at Table 1.[2] For details of artillery equipment, see Appendix D.

Table 1 : Units and Formations of 57 Mountain Division in 1971

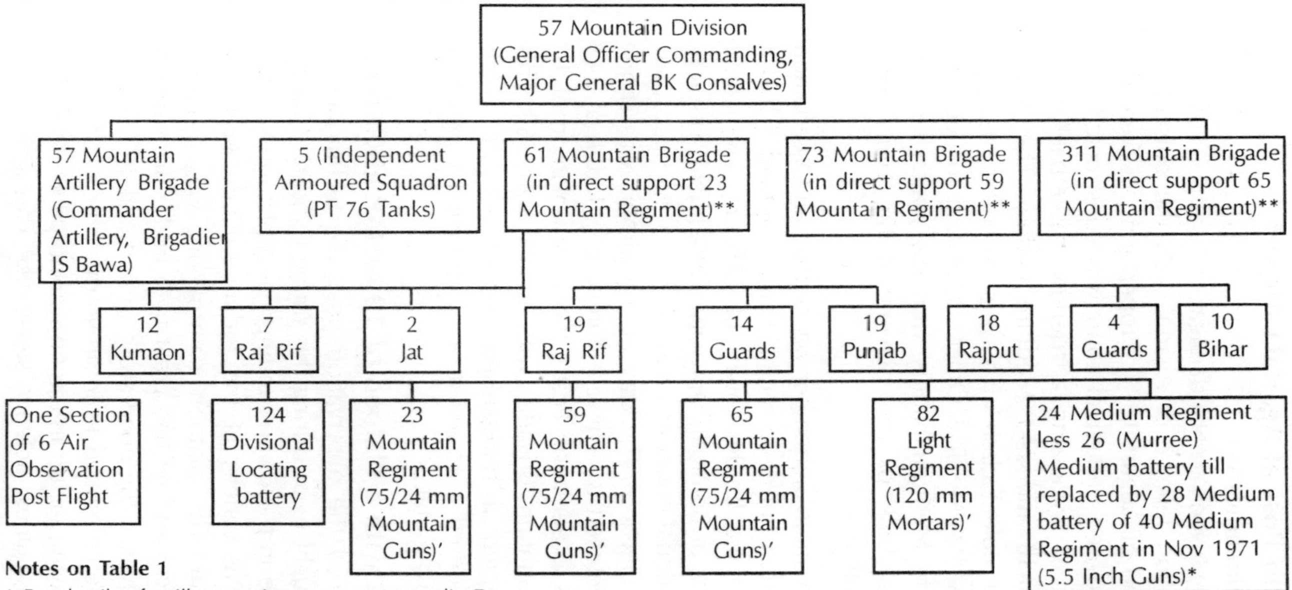

Notes on Table 1

* For details of artillery equipment, see Appendix D.

** Each mountain brigade was given guaranteed firepower, of a close support mountain artillery regiment. In turn, each infantry battalion of a brigade was supported 'in direct support', by mountain battery, which provided observation, communication and liaison, by way of attaching battery Commanders (Major) and two troop commanders (Captains) as Observation Post Officers. The Commanding Officer of the mountain regiment, similarly was affiliated with the brigade commander and at the divisional level, the Commander artillery brigade was Advisor to the General Officer Commanding. This affiliation did not preclude the need for concentration of fire power which is generally done in a planned manner, to derive the maximum shock effect of all guns, within range, accordingly to the tactical situation. Medium and Light Regiment, equipped with 5.5 inch guns, and 120 mm mortars, was similarly deployed for general support, counter-bombardment, and, to add up the firepower. Observation groups of these regiments were deployed to give a wider coverage. The medium battery Commander, as a rule, was in support of armour.

Static Observation Post at Agartala Airport

Regiment Headquarters with 27 (Poonch) and 243 Medium Batteries, were deployed at Nandanagar, in support of 311 Mountain Brigade for defence of Agartala, on the outskirts of Agartala, by the end of August 1971. Proper gun pits were dug and even an improvised basketball court was constructed, and we had the thrill of witnessing a friendly basketball match between 27 (Poonch) and 243 Medium battery. The match turned out to be a violent clash of players. Needless to say, in spite of the Regimental Medical Officer attending to cuts and bruises, 27 (Poonch) Medium battery won the match, as they informed me, that bulk of the players of the unit team, belonged to 27 battery.

My next assignment in September was to man an Observation Post at the Air Traffic Control Tower of Agartala airfield. I had a grandstand view of the border towns of Akhaura, and could also see the outskirts of Brahmanbaria city. The airfield was very close to the international boundary, and 18 Rajput had occupied defences for its protection. The stay at the airport was short-lived. I was then detailed to relieve Lieutenant JS Jodha of 243 Medium battery, as Observation Post Officer with platoon of 10 BIHAR of 311 Mountain Brigade, with a link sign 55.[3] This platoon had occupied a reorganised border outpost which tactically was considered a screen at a place called Gazaria, a few miles South of Agartala.

Observation Post with a Platoon of 10 BIHAR at Gazaria

We had occupied the observation post, the techniques of which had been taught to us during the Young Officer's Course. I was quite at home in these surroundings, as a platoon was the level taught to us as cadets, at the Indian Military Academy (IMA), at Dehradun. The platoon commander was a Junior Commissioned Officer and he had great faith in the fire support my party could deliver, if the need arose (unfortunately I cannot recall his name). We continued to improve our observation post pit and also dug a living shelter in the no war-no peace situation. Due to logistics difficulties, defence stores like corrugated iron

(CGI) sheets and *ballis* (logs of wood) and props were scarce, so we made do with whatever we could improvise.

I had to map-spot the likely Defensive Fire Tasks and pass the coordinates to the gun position. As a raw Second Lieutenant, I carried the first and inaugural edition of the famous 'Blue Book' of the School of Artillery, which had quick and handy references for all information, procedures and fire orders, which an observer may need in battle. I found the chapter on 'Close Target' very mathematical and wondered how did one work out the minute corrections and call for artillery fire, so close to one's own location. A *Machan* was also set up on a tree nearby, and I and my party took turns to occupy it. From the *Machan,* one could have a view of the railway line running from Akhaura, South to Kasba, in East Pakistan. Occasionally, one could hear 105 mm field guns of Pakistan Artillery, firing within their own areas, probably on *Mukti Bahini* targets. My job, as an OP, was also to feed the raw artillery intelligence, in terms of shelling and bombing reports of the Pakistani guns, even if they are not firing at you. These sort of reports help and confirm intelligence gathered from other sources.

The platoon at Gazaria had troops mostly from North Bihar, and our Observation Post party of Sikhs made an interesting combination. The Platoon Havaldar (senior most Non-Commissioned Officer), who was also the platoon Second-in-Command, was Havaldar Tiwari. As he had been a Weapon Training Instructor, I requested him to brush up my weapon training on the carbine. As no firing in retaliation was allowed, it was very difficult to keep our cool, when unseen and hidden Pakistani snipers used to take pot shots on us from across the border. We all got used to 'double bang' of the M-16 rifles of Pakistan Army. The first sound, it is said, is of the bullet crossing the sound barrier near you, and the second sound which immediately follows the first, is the report of Rifle being fired. Soon, we realised that 'double bang' (also referred to as the sound 'tak dhoom') means, one is safe, as one can only hear the sound barrier if one is not hit. Platoon Havaldar Tiwari and I decided that, we must go and investigate and eliminate the sniper by laying an ambush. So the two of us, with a party of two more persons, searched the abandoned village of Etna, which lay across the border. Our patrol was out only for an hour or so, and we could not nab any sniper, though we did see a trench, which had been dug by Pakistani Forces. Later on, learning on this self-styled patrolling, I was warned by my BC, not to undertake independent operations, since everything needed to be coordinated. Since hostilities had not commenced, I could not take the matter in my own hands. Actually, we had not been authorised to take shoots with artillery, on such targets. No artillery fire so far, had been exchanged here. The patrol would not have been given any immediate fire support, as it was not planned. I realised later that, what a mess it would have resulted in. However, it was a good morale booster, for all of us and kept our offensive spirit alive.

The platoon locality was also an important vantage point and very often visitors like Staff Officers from the Mountain Brigade used to visit it to observe across the border. Advanced Position (AP) from 124 Divisional Locating battery was also set up at Gazaria, though no artillery duels ever took place in the sector then. My CO, Lt Col Ashish Banerjee, also visited the OP once, but he concentrated on the sound ranging AP, and its survey. He was quick to check that, not all prismatic compasses were calibrated, after having traversed many longitudes, from where it had been last done (Dehradun). Soon, all of us got assistance to calibrate our compasses. Though it may sound trivial, but even a one degree error can lead to serious inaccuracies and wrong navigation.

During mid-October, we were informed that intelligence sources had indicated a probable Pakistani attack on India. We went on an all-night alert. However, it turned out to be a false alarm. A few days later, two companies of 10 BIHAR, went into retaliatory action, a few miles South of Gazaria, in support of *Mukti Bahini's* operation, to capture Saldanadi. Captain RC Wolfe of 27 (Poonch) Medium battery, and Captain KC Sharma of 243 Medium battery, were detailed as observers with 10 BIHAR and the guns of 65 Mountain Regiment and 243 Medium battery were deployed for the mission. The observation party at Bayek, was under constant medium machine gun fire. In spite of being under fire, registration and adjustments of artillery fire was carried out and fire plan nicknamed *Garam Masala* was executed on the dawn of October 15, 1971. Although, four bunkers were destroyed, the *Mukti Bahini* could not press home the attack, which was called off. 243 Medium battery had fired a total of 346 rounds. Later during the month, further retaliatory operations were progressed at Kasba, which was captured on October 23, 1971, with 243 Medium battery in support. During these operations, 243 Medium battery experienced their first effective counter-bombardment artillery fire by Pakistani gunners, on October 23, 1971. Gunner Narang Singh died instantaneously and two other ranks were injured.

No activity took place across the Gazaria platoon locality, except, for the first time, a lone Pakistani 105 mm gun, fired probably at the post, but luckily for us, the solitary shell whistled past over our location and fell about 300 yards to our rear, on the main road. This was the first enemy artillery fire, in the close vicinity of Agartala, and I, being the closest artillery adviser, was summoned to examine the crater made by the round, to establish the type of weapon used. The brass fuze was recovered from the crater, and I like Sherlock Holmes confidently concluded that, the evidence of a whistling sound of a round in the trajectory, meant that, it was a spinning projectile of a gun and not an unspun mortar bomb, which falls silently like a tear drop. Of course, my 'blue book' came handy, and the crater examination appeared to be accurate. Later, we learnt that, Agartala proper city, was shelled on October 24, 1971. This was the last exciting event and then, I was instructed to join up with the battery, which had already commenced movement southwards with regimental Headquarters to support operations of 23 Mountain Division which was the southern-most division of the IV corps and had a *Murga,* as its formation sign. We called the division, the *'Murga Division'.*

Move to 23 Mountain Division Sector

The outline organisation of formations and units, which comprised 23 Mountain Division is given in Table 2. With effect from October 18, 1971, the battery split into C (Charlie) and D (Delta) troops, each of three guns. C troop with Captain RC Wolfe as Observer, and with me as Gun Position Officer, and Subedar Faqir Singh at the guns, deployed as Tango battery 197 Mountain Regiment, at a place called Garuband, along the Gumti River, 6 kilometres south of Sonamura, to support the defences of 301 Mountain Brigade. No firing was done by C troop. The troop suffered its first casualty, when Lance Naik (Gunner) Gurbhej Singh drowned in river Gumti

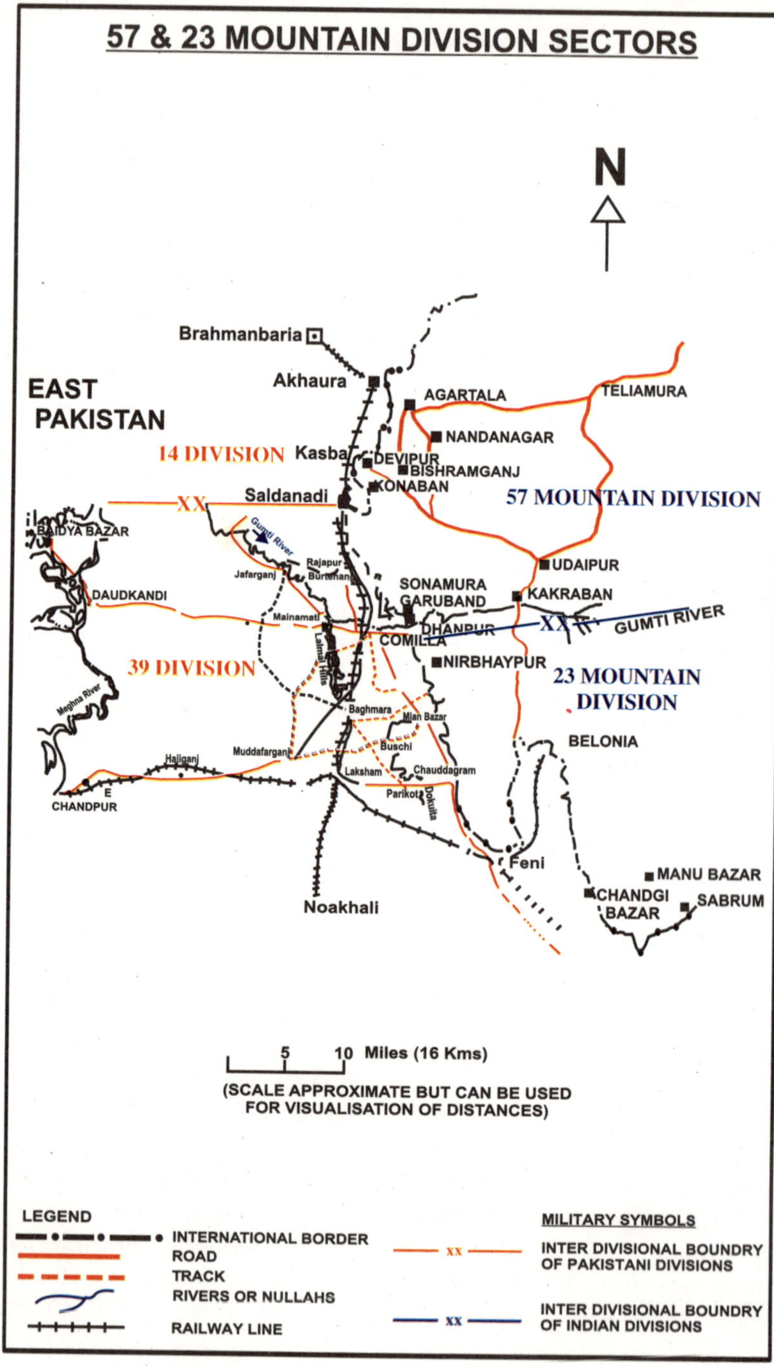
57 & 23 MOUNTAIN DIVISION SECTORS
N
Brahmanbaria
Akhaura
EAST PAKISTAN
AGARTALA
TELIAMURA
NANDANAGAR
14 DIVISION
Kasba
DEVIPUR
BISHRAMGANJ
KONABAN
Saldanadi
57 MOUNTAIN DIVISION
XX
BAIDYA BAZAR
Gumti River
Rajapur
Jafarganj
Burichang
UDAIPUR
DAUDKANDI
SONAMURA
GARUBAND
KAKRABAN
Mainamati
DHANPUR
COMILLA
GUMTI RIVER
NIRBHAYPUR
39 DIVISION
Lalmai Hills
23 MOUNTAIN DIVISION
Meghna River
Baghmara
Mian Bazar
BELONIA
Buschi
Muddafarganj
Hajiganj
Laksham
Chauddagram
CHANDPUR
Parikot
Dokuila
Feni
MANU BAZAR
CHANDGI BAZAR
SABRUM
Noakhali
5 10 Miles (16 Kms)
(SCALE APPROXIMATE BUT CAN BE USED FOR VISUALISATION OF DISTANCES)
LEGEND
INTERNATIONAL BORDER
ROAD
TRACK
RIVERS OR NULLAHS
RAILWAY LINE
MILITARY SYMBOLS
INTER DIVISIONAL BOUNDRY OF PAKISTANI DIVISIONS
INTER DIVISIONAL BOUNDRY OF INDIAN DIVISIONS

Table 2 : Units and Formations of 23 Mountain Division in 1971

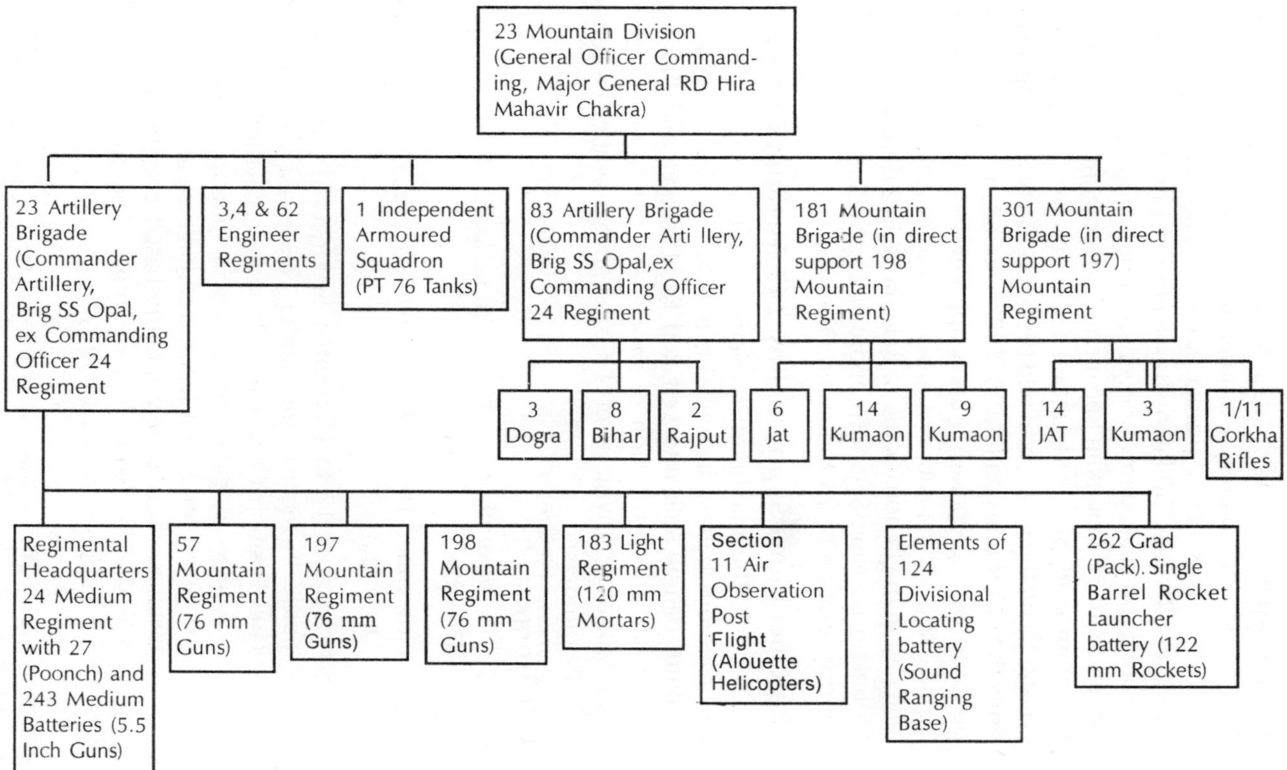

while on a patrol on October 25. Meanwhile, D troop, under Major MC Ramanand, Battery Commander, Captain AR Pedgaonkar, and Naib Subedar Hardip Singh as Gun Position Officer, moved off to Mannu Bazaar, 130 kilometres south of Vishramganj, and fired 49 rounds on vital enemy bridges and ammunition dump as Tango battery, with 57 Mountain Regiment. The moment we came under the command of 23 Mountain Division, we found ourselves constantly on the move, and had the opportunity to fire again (after firing the first rounds on July 28, 1971). Simultaneously, future gun positions were prepared in areas opposite the strong garrisons of Comilla and Maynamati, in areas of Dhanpur. We all were soon to take part in the famous battle of Belonia. Map 2 depicts 57 and 23 Mountain Division Sector in approximate outline. Table 2[4] gives the organisation of 23 Mountain Division.

The Operations Supported by 243 Medium Battery

Perhaps the maximum movement and firing was done by 243 Medium battery in the war, over the 4 Corps sector. 243 Medium battery split into Left and Right troops, and these two troops had the distinction of supporting operations of all the three Mountain Divisions of 4 Corps, in November-December 1971, as under

Left Troop:

(a) Till November 9, 1971: In support of 57 Mountain Division.

(b) November 10 to 17, 1971: In support of 23 Mountain Division.

(c) November 17 to December 5, 1971: The troop moved north, in record time, under Lieutenant VK Gupta, the Gun Position Officer to 8 Mountain Division, as part of 2 Artillery Brigade (which was in support 8 Division, as this division was not tailored to have an artillery brigade, because of its purely infantry-based counter-insurgency role, in the North-East of India). The troop provided fire support to 9 GUARDS at Zakiganj and destroyed one enemy gun in a counter-bombardment role. Later, the troop supported 13 MAHAR and 4 KUMAON of

81 Mountain Brigade, in Kailashahar area, and engaged enemy tanks which were attempting to dislodge a daring road block by 4 KUMAON.[5] Its final location was near Shamsherpur tea gardens, till it was relieved by 26 (Murree) Medium battery.

(d) December 8 onwards, till Ceasefire: Left troop moved South and built up on Right troop at Buschi West of Comilla, and thereafter, 243 Medium battery operated as a whole, in support of 23 Mountain Division.

Right Troop:

(a) Till November 9, 1971: In support of 57 Mountain Division.

(b) November 10 to 27 November, 1971: In support of 23 Mountain Division, including the battle of Belonia, from November 21, onwards.

(c) November 28, 1971 to December 3, 1971: Troop was redeployed at Agartala, a distance of 210 km, which it traversed in record time, and reverted to 57 Mountain Division, to engage counter-bombardment targets, as part of Headquarters 4 Corps Artillery Brigade.

(d) December 4, 1971, onwards till Ceasefire: Troop moved south from Agartala, and joined the Regiment with 27(Poonch) Medium battery and was allotted on priority call to Air Observation Post and also to support advance of 83 Mountain Brigade of 23 Mountain Division.

End Notes

1. *ASLI* is a Hindustani word for 'the real thing' and is used during peace time field firings to differentiate live firing from imaginary firing. *ASLI* during peace time training, means that live ammunition is to be used and all aspects of peace time safety are checked, before *ASLI* is given by the Officer Commanding. *ASLI*, on this day, therefore, implied that we were actually to fire our guns, in a real operation, with live ammunition.

2. For details of all the formations and infantry, armoured, artillery, and engineer units see Jacob, J.F.R, Lt Gen, *Surrender at Dacca: Birth of a Nation,* Manohar Publishers, 1997, Appendix 9. For 57 Mountain Division, see pp. 195-196.

3. These are standard link sign affixed on an artillery radio (wireless) net, to identify commanders, observers and guns. The battery commander is Link Sign 41 and the Observer's Link Sign is 45 and 55, and so on.

4. Jacob, op. cit. For 23 Mountain Division, see pp. 194-195.

5. See Praval K.C.: *Valour Triumphs: A History of the Kumaon Regiment.,* Thomson Press (India) Ltd, 1976, pp. 312-313. In the mid-1990s, I met my coursemate, Brigadier Jasbir Singh, who was a Second Lieutenant in 4 Kumaon, and he recalled the action of his battalion and the fire support of the medium guns. He is now writing *The History of* 4 *Kumaon* (forthcoming).

4

The Battles of Belonia Bulge : November 1971

By the beginning of November 1971, the personnel of the battery had become experts in movement of the heavy gun-kraz train, over narrow tracks and culverts. Weak bridges as a drill, were negotiated after unhooking the gun with the tractor and manhandling the gun to reduce the combined load of both the gun and the tower on the culvert or bridge. The engineers had improved certain patches, and rafts were constructed for us to cross the smaller rivers. But the best solution to negotiate boggy patches of ground, was the 'Wheel Mat', made of cane, about 6 feet by 4, and the skill of the Kraz driver. As we moved towards Belonia, a cyclone had hit the coastal areas in the Bay of Bengal and there was heavy rainfall, making the vehicles sink in the marshy terrain. We somehow managed to push through, using all ingenious means like winching, heaving and preparation of 'rush jobs' on our own. Being the only medium gunners in the sector, we were generally given the right of passage on various tracks, by the military police, something only flag officers, like the GOC, used to get.

During the month of November, 23 Mountain Division undertook the preliminary operation, by capturing the Belonia Bulge [1], which was south-east of Laksham. It was shaped like a tongue or bulge, 25 kilometres long, and about 10 kilometres wide, jutting into Tripura (See Map 3).

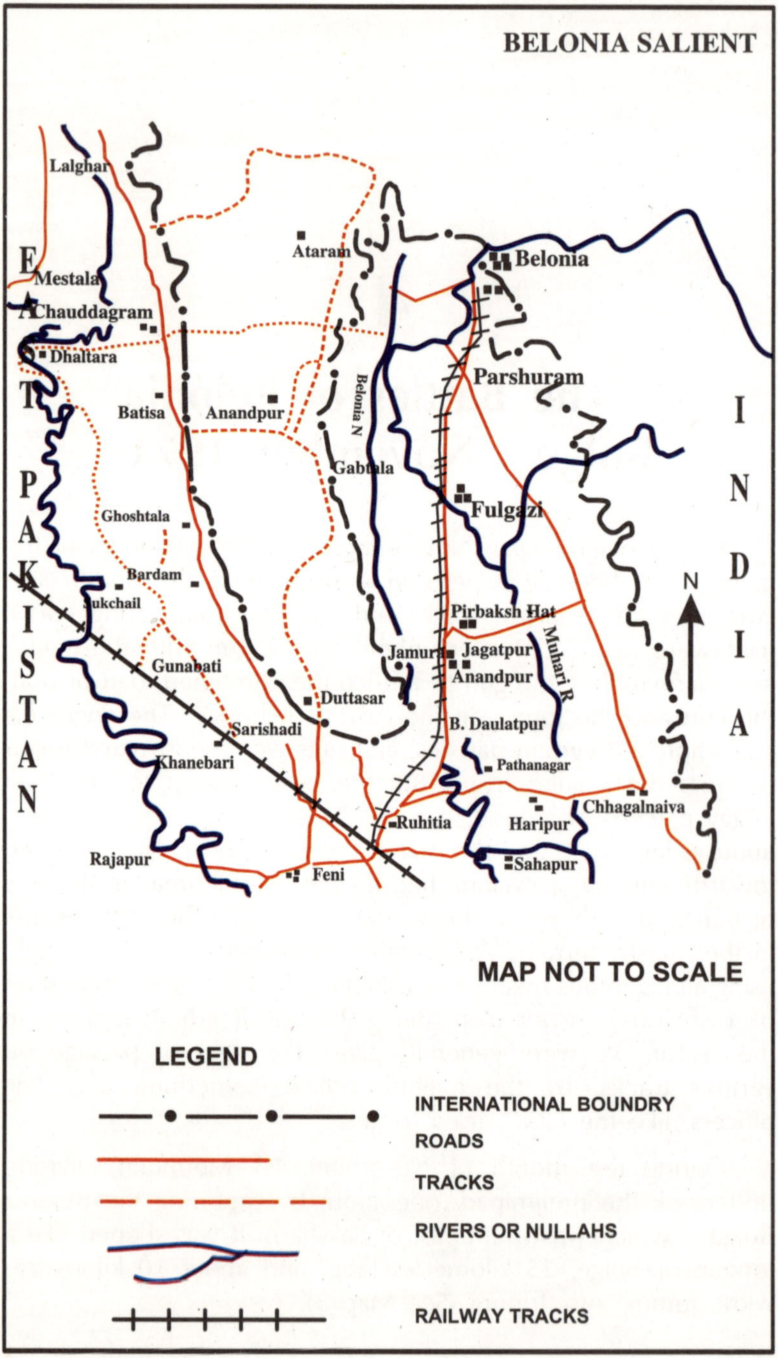
BELONIA SALIENT
Lalghar
Mestala
Chauddagram
Dhaltara
Batisa
Anandpur
Ataram
Belonia
Parshuram
Belonia N
Gabtala
Fulgazi
Ghoshtala
Bardam
Sukchail
Pirbaksh Hat
Muhari R
Jamura
Jagatpur
Anandpur
Gunabati
Duttasar
B. Daulatpur
Sarishadi
Pathanagar
Khanebari
Chhagalnaiva
Ruhitia
Haripur
Sahapur
Rajapur
Feni
EAST PAKISTAN
INDIA
N
MAP NOT TO SCALE
LEGEND
INTERNATIONAL BOUNDRY
ROADS
TRACKS
RIVERS OR NULLAHS
RAILWAY TRACKS

The deployment of Pakistani Forces at this point of time was that an adhoc 39 Infantry Division had been raised and located at Chandpur, which was a major and southern-most ferry site, on the Meghna River. 39 Division was responsible for the defence of the area east of Meghna from Saldanadi to the border with Burma. Towards the north, the Gumti River was the inter-divisional boundary with Pakistan's 14 Infantry Division, which was responsible for areas from Akhaura-Brahmanbaria,. till Sylhet. The brigades of 39 Infantry Division were :

(a) **117 Brigade (Brigadier Shiekh Mansoor Hussain Atif), Headquarters at Comilla** :

(i) 30 PUNJAB. Saldanadi to Mian Bazar.

(ii) 25 Frontier Force (FF). Mian Bazar, Lalmaki to Daudkandi.

(iii) 23 PUNJAB. Comilla to Chaudagram.

(iv) 53 Field Regiment in support with 105 mm guns (13 guns).

(b) **53 Brigade (Brig Aslam Niazi) Headquarters at Feni and responsible for Chaudagram, Feni and Belonia with:**

(i) 15 BALUCH (In Belonia Bulge).

(ii) 39 BALUCH.

(iii) 21 Azad Kashmir (AK) 1 Coy.

The area of operation in Belonia, therefore, were having the Baluch battalions. Initially, 83 Mountain Brigade was given the task to capture the border outposts of Belonia and Parshuram, for which D troop deployed in Belonia on November 2, 1971, and thereafter, the battery got intimately involved in these preliminary operations as a part of 23 Mountain Division. First of all Captain AR Pedgaonkar and Captain RC Wolfe got detached immediately as Observation Post Officers with 83 Mountain Brigade/3 DOGRA. Observation Post parties of 57 Mountain Regiment in direct support to 83 Mountain Brigade had already joined up with Infantry. A single gun of Havaldar Mohinder Singh-70 was deployed 10 kilometres further to the south on south on the tip of Belonia finger, to reach out at depth-targets like enemy concentrations, bridges and railway tracks. Orders were then received by the C troop to redeploy and build up on D troop. Heavy cyclonic and torrential rains lashed the area and C troop deployed at Garuband near Sonamura took nearly five hours to get out of the gun position as the ground became soggy and a quagmire of mud. In spite of unfavourable weather, the troops were in high spirit as we had not fired our guns since July and we were looking forward to some action now. On the morning of November 6, C Troop reached the vicinity of Belonia Bulge after covering 110 kilometres. Orders were received to quickly deploy the guns to engage enemy activities. However as the ground was soft the very first guns sank into the ground and two Krazes got bogged down on the berms of the road causing a traffic jam. Fortunately the third Kraz had not got stuck and it was skilfully used to recover the other two guns and Krazes. By dusk the first gun of C troop pulled out from the slush managed to reach D troop location and came into action with the two guns of D troop. By the next morning on November 7, 1971, the remaining two guns of C troop could reach D troop gun area. Meanwhile, two guns of D troop and the single gun of Havaldar Mohinder Singh-70 were engaging impromptu and opportunity targets. In the evening orders were received for the two guns of C troop to pull out and build up ahead on the single gun of D troop. C troop reached the next gun area a distance of 7 kilometres to the south at 0400h (4 in the morning) of November 8, 1971. This was the third gun area in two days. Now the battery had finally deployed in two troops in support of our operations at the Belonia Bulge. Captain AR Pedgaonkar moved with 3 DOGRA of 83 Mountain Brigade, as Link sign 45, and Captain RC Wolfe to 2 RAJPUT of 83 Mountain Brigade. Other observation post parties were provided by 57 Mountain Regiment and 1833 Light battery of 183 Light Regiment. As soon as C troop reported ready on November 8, 1971, an enemy train coming up on metre gauge railway line Feni-Fulgazi-Belonia was engaged by Major Avtar Singh of 57 Mountain Regiment, as an observer with the guns of the battery. The shoot was effective as the train had been hit and derailed and thus the enemy could not get forward its reinforcements.

Meanwhile, Captain AR Pedgaonkar effectively registered targets with both C and D troops.

Capture of Parshuram by 3 DOGRA (November 8,1971)

Simultaneous to these moves and deployments during early November 1971 the border outpost of Belonia was captured by 2 RAJPUT of 83 Mountain Brigade, with elements of *Mukti Bahini.* It was then decided to capture the next enemy border outpost at Parshuram by 3 DOGRA of 83 Mountain Brigade. We had been taught the mechanics of execution of a fire plan, during our Young Officers' Course. Getting a real target list with a task table to provide covering fire to our Infantry had an electrifying effect on the gunners. More so, as the medium Forward Observation Officer (FOO), (the term used when an Observation Post Officer goes in assault), was none other than our own Captain AR Pedgaonkar. Targets were registered by firing, while the fire plan nicknamed 'Dam Busters', was received. Technical work in all respects was completed before dusk or last light*. Just before H Hour we heard bangs of our own heavy mortars of 183 Light Regiment followed by the drumbeat sound of the mountain guns of 57 Mountain Regiment, and then, it was our turn. Firing was synchronised to ensure that the opening rounds from all artillery guns and batteries land simultaneously on the targets. The shooting was effective and we could hear the battle cry of 3 DOGRA, in the far distance. After having fired 80 rounds, we heard the crackle on the radio, to inform us that the attack was successful, and Captain AR Pedgaonkar had personally captured one Medium Machine gun.[2] By now we had fired 400 rounds in Belonia Sector.

November 9 to 14, 1971

After the capture of Parshuram, 27 (Poonch) Medium battery reverted to its general support and interdiction role. On November 9, the Air Observation Post (I think he was Major or Captain Sihota, who later became an Army Commander), took effective shoots on an enemy gun area. At 1500 hrs (3 pm),

* Technical and tactical gunnery is a science, as it is an art. For interest of gunners and readers having inclination for gunnery, some interesting gunnery problems encountered are given in Appendix E.

four Pakistani Sabre jets were seen ahead, at the forward line of defences. The forward troops (2 RAJPUT) were straffed and rocketed. Subedar Faqir Singh recalled the stories of 1965 war when air attacks by Sabre jet on our gun area had killed Captain Khola of the Regiment. The next day (November 10, 1971), C troop again fired on enemy concentrations. For two hours an enemy Air Observation Aircraft (Bird Dog) flew over the area, and at 1500 hrs (3 pm), again the four eagle-like Sabre jets were seen. This time, two of them took a circuit over C troop gun area, but nothing happened. Apparently, the guns had not been spotted by them. We could see the puffs of anti-aircraft shells, as the aircraft were engaged by the troop of 48 Air Defence Regiment, who reportedly caused damage to three aircraft.** Thereafter, we did not see any more enemy Sabre jets. On November 10,1971, C troop gun area was shelled in the evening with 105 mm guns of the enemy for about 10 minutes. We had no casualties. Later in the day our ground Observation Post spotted an enemy gun area which was immediately engaged by C Troop by firing 85 rounds. The shelling was effective since a lot of vehicles were seen rushing out of the gun area and the enemy guns went silent. During this time we also got information that on November 10, 1971, one of the 1 ton vehicles belonging to 57 Mountain Regiment, with the Mike Party (Line Laying Party), had received a direct hit from a stray enemy artillery round killing the detachment of four and wounding another four. Such is the fate and destiny which artillery delivers.

** The history of the Regiment of Artillery *Gods of War* records, at page 340, that one F-86 was shot down by C Troop of 178 Air Defence (AD) battery of 48 Air Defence Regiment. The History of the 1971 Indo Pakistan War of the Ministry of Defence, which was placed in public domain, via the internet (see bibliography) in 2001, on page 234, mentions that "soon after the capture of Belonia Railway Station by 2 Rajput and the BSF, four Pak Sabre jets strafed Indian troops on November 9, when one of them was damaged by MMG fire from 3 Dogra. Next day, four Sabres came again and strafed Indian positions, but three of them were damaged by Indian Air Defence guns". It is not unusual to have conflicting claim in air defence operations. Till this book went to press, the history of the Rajput Regiment had not been published.

Deception Plans of the Battery level

The communication centre at Laksham (See Map 2) was a strong position, under the responsibility of Pakistan 53 Brigade. Laksham was on the main approach to Chandpur. If Laksham was strongly held, a swift advance to Chandpur would have been a difficult task. However, if somehow, the enemy was made to believe that the main thrust would be on Feni in the South, it was appreciated that it may pull out troops from Laksham and reinforce Feni. Dovetailed with the preliminary captures of Belonia and Parshuram it was intended to give an impression that Feni and areas to its south were the main areas of our interest. Besides the capture of the Belonia Bulge (given later) radio deception was also employed.[3] A phantom radio-net was established to simulate fake signal traffic. To give authenticity to this phantom-net of a division a single gun of Havaldar Kehar Singh under myself as Gun Position Officer, was deployed 10 kilometres south of C troop gun area near the tip of Belonia finger. Captain AR Pedgaonkar who had since joined 14 KUMAON of 181 Mountain Brigade was the static Observation Post Officer. He engaged a total of five targets of which one was the airfield at Feni—where an air observation post aircraft was seen landing. The shooting was effective and call signs of a divisional artillery were used on the radio for deception purposes. Meanwhile, C and D troops fired 50 rounds, during the course of the day. The single gun after taking part in this deception plan was pulled back and redeployed with C troop.

Operation Sultana, November 16-17, 1971

An estimated company of enemy was reported in an area called Nilaki which was earlier with the *Mukti Bahini* on the western side of the Belonia Bulge. It was planned to capture Nilaki by 14 KUMAON battalion of 181 Mountain Brigade in order to threaten the western flank of the enemy at Fulgazi in the Belonia Bulge. Major MC Ramanand and Captain AR Pedgaonkar moved out with the battalion as link sign 41 and 45. Captain AR Pedgaonkar was again the medium Forward Observation Officer (FOO) with Captain VK Kalia as the direct support FOO, from 57 Mountain Regiment. Registration of targets was done by firing and at 2000 hrs, on November 16, 1971, the guns of 27 (Poonch) Medium battery and two batteries of 57 Mountain Regiment fired on fire plan 'Fire Correct'. The attacking troops were pinned down under heavy medium machine gun fire and the attack could not be launched.[4] This was the first unsuccessful attack, and I can recall vividly, when the observation post officers called for stopping artillery fire on the radio net as own and enemy fires had come very close to the troops in or ahead of the forming up place. The whole night there were artillery duals with C and D troops firing 110 and 40 rounds respectively. In the early morning of November 17, 1971, the enemy started heavy shelling of the pinned down troops and attempted to launch a counter-attack. At this stage Captain AR Pedgaonkar came out from his trench to have better observation in order to engage the enemy with artillery fire. An airburst shell of 105 mm howitzer of Pakistan Artillery burst just over his position killing him on the spot. At 0900 hrs the Air Observation Post and the ground observer Major Avtar Singh the Battery Commander of 57 Mountain Regiment again engaged pre-recorded targets and likely gun areas and a total of 60 rounds were fired. The body of Captain AR Pedgaonkar was recovered and brought back by Havaldar Kabal Singh who had been detailed for the task. He was cremated in the wagon lines {Administrative area)‡‡. The same day two L60 40 mm BOFOR

‡‡ Cremation of the dead was done as soon as possible, in the wagon lines or in the vicinity, during tactical pauses. The remains of the dead, as ashes, were preserved and later delivered to the next of kin, after the war. A tough and a sensitive job. This is in contrast to what the Government decided from 1999, during the limited border skirmish with Pakistan at Kargil, when the bodies were flown back to the home town of martyred soldiers to be cremated with full militay honours. It was probably to make a national event out of it. When possible, say in low intensity conflict or other such missions, this may be welcome, but in a. general war, it is unlikely that there would be a possibility of arranging air transport and other administrative arrangements, to send a body back. By field level cremation, under the Religious Teacher, near the battlefield, the unit personnel were intimately involved in the ceremony, and the cremation was also considered a solemn unit family affair.

guns of 48 Air Defence Regiment were deployed with C and D troops respectively, for air defence. On November 18, 1971, C troop pulled out and built up with D troop, the battery was together after 29 days, and Captain RC Wolfe returned back to the battery for a temporary period. It has been said that war is full of lulls and boredom. November 19 was one such day as only one round was fired by the battery. We took advantage of this peaceful day and had quick baths in succession, next to our camouflaged command post. A few troops took a hair wash which was badly needed.

Operation Harvest: The Final Clearance of the Bulge

In the operations so far undertaken by 83 Mountain Brigade, the areas upto south of Parshuram were taken over by us and the line of control cut across from east to west just north of Fulgazi which was under the control of Pakistan Army. The enemy in the south half of the remaining bulge comprised 15 and 39 BALUCH, one battalion East Pakistan Civil Armed Police (EPCAF), a few light tanks, one field battery and one section mortars.[5] It was decided to trap the enemy between forward defence lines and Feni by advance of 83 and 181 Mountain Brigades from East and West and link-up astride the railway line.[6] For this operation Major MC Ramanand moved out as medium Battery Commander with 1 (Independent) Armoured Squadron of 7 CAVALRY which was operating under command of 181 Mountain Brigade with PT 76 Tanks (the engine of this tank was the same fitted on the Kraz). Captain RC Wolfe moved out as Observer with 2 RAJPUT and myself as a Medium Observation Post Officer with D Coy of 6 JAT, the company under the able command of Major 55 Bhuttar. * Due to paucity

---

* *The History of the Jat Regiment,* Volume III by Gautam Sharma does not record the pre-December operations unlike other Regimental histories (see bibliography). Major HB Kala who was a senior major and was probably the second-in-command, later retired as an Army Commander. I met him after the war, as General Officer Commanding Army Training Command in 1999, at School of Artillery together with the then Adjutant Captain PS Rautela who as a Colonel was on his staff.

and heavy demand on the only medium battery for fire requests, the deployment per force was done together as a battery for administrative reasons but both C and D troops were given separate tasks. C troop with Subedar Faqir Singh as Gun Position Officer was in direct support of 1 (Independent) Armoured Squadron and D troop was in support of Infantry and for counter-bombardment tasks.

My old static Observation Post Party personnel of October 1971 (with 10 BIHAR at Gazaria) were detailed to accompany me. They were a solid team—the main radio operator who could lift his booster set like a play ball with ease was Harbhajan Singh, thoroughly cool-headed, strong and fearless. Then, there was the Technical Assistant Surender Singh, short, sturdy and alert, and finally my batman-cum-second radio operator, Sher Singh. We bade farewell to the gunners at the gun end and were dropped in a 1 ton truck to join with 6 JAT. We reached the assembly area and I located Major RI Subramaniyam[7] the direct support battery Commander of 198 Mountain Regiment with 6 JAT. He welcomed me to his team and I was given the link sign 105 on radio, as a Medium Observation Post Officer. The jat troops were quite surprised and happy to have a light weight as a medium observer who could control the heaviest shell of 80 pounds in the theatre of war. I was impressed with the infantry battalion's *esprit-de-corps* and offensive spirit. Also with the battalion was Major Khalid Musharraf of *Mukti Bahini*, dressed in jeans and shirt, with an impressive beard. He was leading his *Mukti Bahini* forces which were attached in about a company strength, with each Indian infantry battalion. The plan as I understood as a subaltern was simple. Two brigades from divergent axis were to advance to infiltrate from vertically opposite directions and join up to create a massive block to trap the enemy troops in the Belonia Bulge. The bulk of artillery including 27 Medium Battery was deployed on the west of the Bulge, so it implied that technically, 6 JAT and other troops would be advancing into the line of fire (See Map 4).

BROAD DEPLOYMENT IN BELONIA SALIENT : OPERATION HARVEST

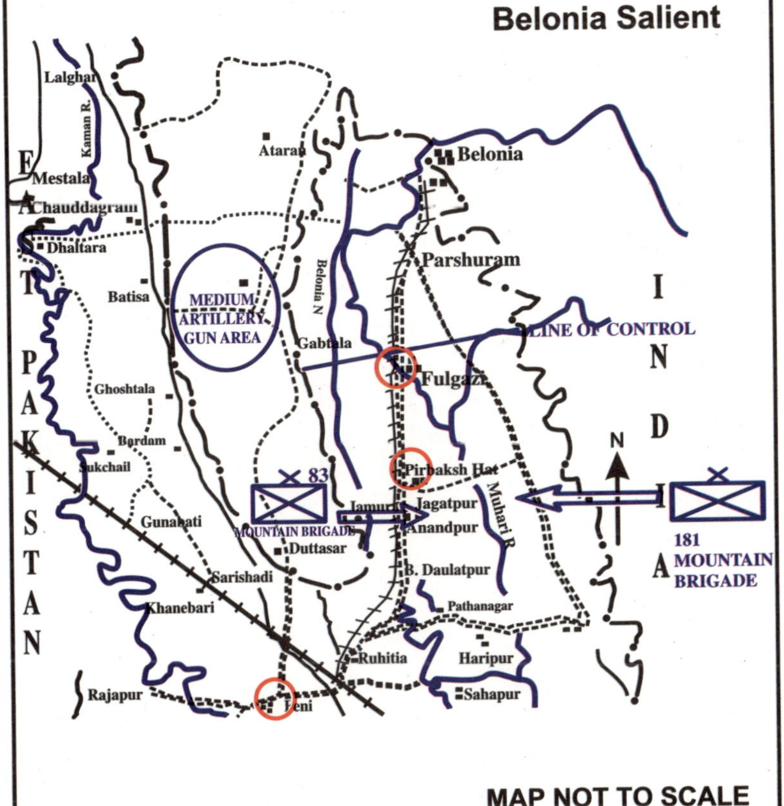

LEGEND

1. BLUE REPRESENTS INDIA FORCES
2. RED REPRESENTS PAKISTANI ARMY DISPOSITONS (APPROXIMATE)
3. NOT TO SCALE AND APPROXIMATE DISPOSITION ARE SHOWN

THE PROBLEM OF ADVANCING INTO THE LINE OF FIRE AT BELONIA (PLAN VIEW)

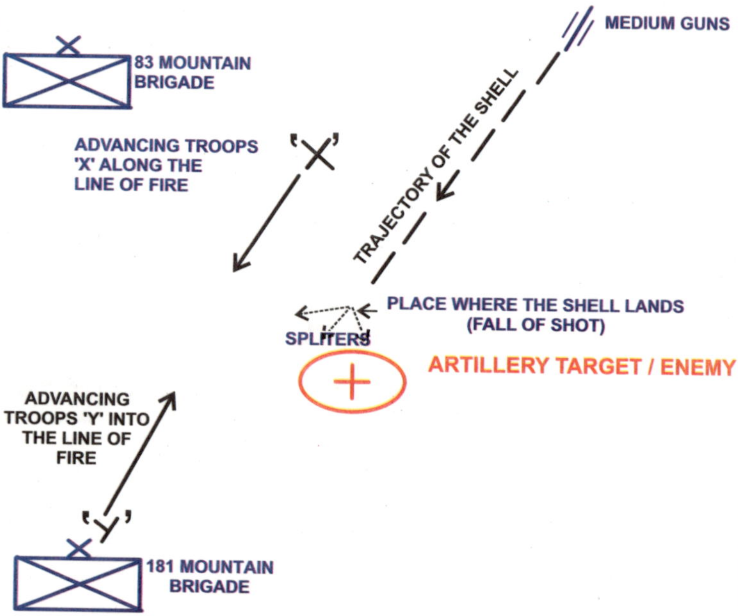

ADVANCING TROOPS 'X' CAN COME CLOSER TO THE FALL OF SHOT WITH GREATER EASE THAN TROOPS 'Y' WHO HAVE TO MAINTAIN GREATER DISTANCE FROM FALL OF SHOT

Now, in gunnery, generally during training and peace time field firing restrictions, one is used to seeing guns firing from behind, and the rounds go over the troops and land ahead. The shells and the splinters have tendency to go ahead - away from one, and towards the target, and it is easier and safer to come as close as daringly possible to the fall of shot of a round which is fired from behind. However, once guns are firing into you, along the line of fire, and you approach from the opposite direction, safety aspect gets enhanced, as the rounds / splinters along the trajectory can hit one from a great distance, when compared to advancing with overhead fire. I revised the various technical procedure that I may have to undertake, if at all I was to take a shoot as a Medium Forward Observation Officer in support of 6 JAT, in close proximity of friendly forces, with the guns firing into you (see Sketch 1).

I, with my party, reported to Maj SS Bhuttar, the daring and lean company commander of D Company. We were welcomed warmly by him and I soon became a part of his company headquarters with my party. As we were a unit of Sikh troops, who wear a *pugree,* (turban), we had very few World War I—solid pattern helmets of the British (Post Box) pattern, meant for issue to non-Sikhs, who were mostly officers. I found that the Infantry had a better looking and lighter pattern helmet, which was called the 'Naidu' pattern of helmets, akin to the US Army design. I realised that I was the odd man out in this helmet (but the stuff it was made of could easily deflect the fastest splinter). On the evening of November 22, we set off in a single file, D Company leading, guided by the *Mukti Bahni* scouts, along a cross-country approach. No opposition was encountered, till suddenly, after two hours or so, at about 2100 hrs (9 pm), we heard a muffled battle cry and found heavy automatic fire from our left, as it was pitch dark and we could hear bullets whiz past us, overhead, and also hear their sound of hitting trees. The Company Commander immediately assessed the situation and ordered his company to hit the ground, without opening fire. I was impressed with the command and control, and the men of D Company, 6 JAT, obeyed the instructions without any noise or confusion in the pitch of the night and took cover. We soon realised that the enemy party which fired on us was a stray jitter party on a patrol and we had not been effectively ambushed as we had no casualties. Had not the company commander ordered his troops to lie low, without opening fire, it could have been that, our troops could have got involved in cross-fire with one another. In any case, I could not have engaged such a close target with artillery, as the rounds would have endangered own troops. It was a real practical lesson of fire control which is vital in any tactical action. After advancing for about four to five kilometres, the battalion halted and firmed in, while the next battalion (14 KUMAON) took the lead. As enemy 105 mm guns were firing at random into our general area, and though no casualties were being caused, it was decided that I, as a Medium Observation Post Officer, must sort out the 105 mm guns. I was instructed to engage the enemy guns. Now, to engage enemy guns is one thing, but to find out its coordinates to a reasonable degree of accuracy, at night, without the aid of sophisticated instruments, is another. Generally, the sound ranging devices can obtain location of such hostile batteries, using acoustic means and then our guns retaliate. As the fire is not observed (there are no human observers to correct the misses and report the hits), great care is taken in finding the ballistic, meteorological and survey conditions, in order to ensure that this predicated fire lands to a reasonable degree of accuracy and neutralises the intended target. However, as sound ranging devices were not available, I decided that in such situation, most of the elementary methods are also acceptable. So I plotted the bearing of the flash of enemy guns on my map and judged the distance to approximate 7000 yards or so. Having read off the grid reference using a shaded torch from my map, I passed my maiden fire orders to C Troop to engage enemy guns.

At the gun end, the Regimental Command Post with the Adjutant was also deployed and since the Adjutant Captain BCS Jagati was the control station, he was updated on the overall macro level picture of the operations; counter-bombardment being one such facet. Being at the hub of command and communications, the Adjutant of an artillery regiment is updated on the tactical picture for the entire division in near real time. To exercise control over ammunition, it is normal in any operation, to lay down restrictions on the number of rounds to be fired. When the Adjutant heard my fire request on the radio to C Troop he contacted the Gun Position Officer Naib Subedar Hardip Singh, and ordered him (according to his judgment) not to engage the enemy guns, as it was a waste of ammunition, due to tactical and technical reasons. Now, I was oblivious to these happenings, and soon heard C Troop giving the report that 9 rounds per gun had been fired, sweeping and searching an area of 200 yards by 200 yards—as this information was passed to the Infantry, I could see the electrifying effect on morale and my party got truly recognised as a medium observation post party. Fortunately, the enemy guns played up and became silent, though, it could have been due to reasons other than accurate fire by us. This was a classic example of turning a 'Nelson's Eye'[8] by Naib Subedar Hardip Singh, in that, he had informed the Adjutant that as the Gun Position Officer (now with the infantry as Observation Post Officer) of the battery had asked for fire, fire he would and he did. The Adjutant, of course, on reconsideration, had the magnanimity to be very proud of the spirit displayed by Naib Subedar Hardip Singh, and the matter was happily closed.

During the late hours of the night of November 22/23, 1971, the Pakistani troops were quick to withdraw and get out of the trap. According to Major General Sukhwant Singh, in his book *Liberation of Bangladesh,* the Pakistani forces withdrew with guns and equipment, through a gap not more than 2000 yards, between the two road blocks of 83 and 181 Mountain Brigades.[9] The townships of Fulgazi and Pir Baksh Hat, were in our hands on November 23, 1971. During the day of November 23, 1971, Major MC Ramanand, the battery Commander, engaged the enemy on the run with C troop. 6 JAT, thereafter, followed the wake of 14 KUMAON which had overrun an enemy position, suffering some casualties, including one mine casualty. D Company 6 JAT was ordered to take over the captured post at Jagatpur. On the track, leading to the piece of high ground, where Pakistani defence had been captured, a box of anti-personnel mines was found, with two of the mines missing. As one mine casualty had been caused earlier in 14 KUMAON, it was deduced by D Company of 6 JAT, that the second mine could be buried or scattered by the withdrawing enemy. There was no engineer or personnel from the pioneer platoon, however the Company had one young Junior Commissioned Officer, who had recently done the field engineering course at the College of Military Engineering at Poona, and he took out his bayonet and commenced plodding systematically, and soon, he recovered a cunningly camouflaged mine, which added up to the total content of the box. This mine clearing operation impressed me most. The company followed through the cleared track and occupied defences which were the Line of Control. Tanks of 1 (Independent) Armoured Squadron and other infantry units continued to have some skirmishes during November 23 to 24[10] and later, till the end of November.[11] By November 24 Chandgi Bazaar was abandoned by the enemy which marked the end of this operation.[12] The battery had fired 180 rounds in this operation. Before moving out of the sector, selected gunners visited a few erstwhile target areas and saw a train derailed, and a pockmarked enemy gun area, which had one parapet of a gun pit blown off, evidently with the direct hits scored by the gunners—the shooting had been very effective and accurate. Two personal experiences during the Belonia Operation, are worth recounting. First was that, on the day of the air attack ahead of the gun position, the 'Pay Parade' was also in progress. It was a novel experience to count and distribute pay from slit trenches. In any case, the battery head clerk (unfortunately I cannot recall his name) was mighty pleased, as our acquaintance rolls tallied with the cash distributed, and we could send the document to our Headquarters, within 24 hours, according the financial rules. The second was that, during mid-November, I received a parcel from my mother, which was a book, titled *Autobiography of a*

Yogi by Paramahansa Yogananda (Bombay : Jaico Publishers). Though I could never get time to read the book then, nevertheless, it found a right place in my haversack (Pack 08), which I used to use as a briefcase. Surely, the spiritual vibrations and message of self-realisation must have given me energy to perform the job at hand, to the best of my ability.

End Notes

1. Jagdev Singh, Brigadier, AVSM. *Dismemberment of Pakistan, 1971-Indo-Pakistan* Lancer International, 1988 p.107. When I was posted at the School of Artillery, in Devlali in 1998 Major Naser Ahmed from the Bangladesh Army who was my student mentioned that in the Staff College in Bangladesh the battles of Belonia is a case study for the students in the curriculum.
2. Palsukar RD, Colonel, Vir Chakra. *The DOGRA Regiment, A Saga of Gallantry and Valour. Historical Record* (1858-1981). Published under arrangements Commandant, Dogra Regimental Centre, Faizabad (1982). Details of the battalion history of 3 DOGRA are given in this historical digest. Two other ranks were killed and six were wounded. The Pakistani garrison had 28 killed and 55 wounded or taken prisoners.
3. Sukhwant Singh, Major General. *The Liberation of Bangladesh* Vikas Publishing House Pvt Ltd, 1981, p.152. The author was the Deputy Director General at Directorate General of Military Operations, Army Headquarters. He had listed out four deception measures to lure Pakistani 53 Infantry Brigade from Laksham to Feni and these were:
   (a) Roads and bridges from Shanti Bazaar to Sabrum were improved to indicate Indian interest at Feni.
   (b) Administrative activity was stepped up.

(c) Phantom radio network simulating formation level traffic was established.

(d) Preliminary operations were carried out.

4. Praval KC. *Valour Triumphs: A History of The Kumaon Regiment.* Thomson Press (India) Limited, 1976, pp. 311-312. The details of this action of the 14 KUMAON battalion have been covered in the Regimental History. The battalion lost 10 other ranks killed and 32 wounded.
5. Jagdev Singh. op. cit, p.107.
6. Sukhwant Singh, op. cit, p.153.
7. He was a former young officer of 24 Medium Regiment and was the Survey Officer during the 1965 War. Later, he was posted to 198 Mountain Regiment.
8. The expression 'Nelson's Eye' is derived from the exploits of Hortio Nelson (1758-1805) of British Navy. He had lost an arm and right eye during various engagements. In an attack on Danish Ships off Copenhagen, Nelson was the Second-in-Command. The British found it difficult to fight the enemy. Nelson, when signaled to stop, put the telescope to his blind eye and said that he could not 'see' the signal and continued the battle which he won. Naib Subedar Hardip Singh, in his own way, repeated the act, which can be called 'Turning a Hardip's Eye'.
9. Sukhwant Singh. op. cit, p.153.
10. Proudfoot, Lt Col (Retd.) Editor, *WE LEAD: 7TH LIGHT CAVALRY 1784-1990/* Lancer International, 1991, pp. 204-205. Operations of 1 (Independent) Armoured Squadron with 9 KUMAON have been covered and it has been mentioned that the squadron had crossed the border and was recalled temporarily, had it not been for this delay, they would have captured a battery of Pakistani Artillery and Brigadier

Aslam Khan Niazi, with his order group, the brigade commander of 53 Pak brigade. Later, 181 Mountain Brigade with 198 Mountain Regiment cleared enemy forces at Mridaya Bazar and Matua.

11. Palsukar RD, Col, MC, *The Bihar Warriors: Historical Records of Bihar Regiment* 1986. For operations of 8 BIHAR of 83 Mountain Brigade, see pp. 256-258.

12. Harbans Singh, Major (Retd),PSC, *Battle Honours of the Indian Army,* Vision Books, 1993, p. 264. 2 RAJPUT was awarded the Battle Honour of Belonia.

5

The December 1971 War

Plans Before the Battle

After the battle experiences of Belonia, the battery was ordered to move back to its main gun area at Dhanpur to be able to support the Comilla Sector of Pakistani Forces. The battery Commander and Observation Post parties returned to the gun position, temporarily. Captain RS Sandhu joined us on posting from Artillery Centre, Nasik, as the Senior Observation Post Officer; with him also came many reservists, who were on reserve liability. The strength of the battery was nearly complete, the reservists, who were mostly truck or taxi drivers, as civilians, had lost touch with the finer aspects of handling guns and other equipment, but were a great help in transporting of ammunition and giving heaves and pushes to bogged down guns or vehicles, contributing with real 'manpower'. The battery then was all set for the war to break out and awaited the expected and set piece battle of the capture of Comilla-Maynamati complex. But, as it generally happens in war, without firing a round, to achieve surprise, we moved down south,. 20 kilometres to Kalkrishnagar (KK Nagar), on December 2. The reconnaissance party came under some stray shelling and as usual, both the troops deployed together, C troop for counter-bombardment and D troop for support to the infantry and armour. Major MC Ramanand moved off to 1 (Independent) Armoured Squadron, as Link Sign 41, Captain RS Sandhu with 1/11 Gorkha Rifles of 301 Mountain Brigade as Link Sign 45, and Captain RC Wolfe with 83 Mountain Brigade as Link Sign 55. I was the Gun Position Officer of C troop and Naib Subedar Hardip Singh was with D troop. The Regimental Headquarters was also deployed next to the battery. Right troop of 243 Medium battery, under Major S Jadhav and Subedar Ran Singh also joined us after support of 57 Mountain Division. The Left troop of 243 Medium battery, had moved northwards out of 57 Mountain Division, in opposite direction, on the night of November 27/28, to Karimganj and Kailashahar, to support operations of 8 Mountain Division, for the capture of Zakiganj on November 30, 1971, in Sylhet sector. Then, as 26 (Murree) Medium battery with five guns reached 8 Mountain Division on December 3/4,1971, from opposite the Chinese Sector of Sela in NEFA, the Left troop of 243 Medium battery moved back overnight on December 5, 1971, under Second Lieutenant VK Gupta to join with Right troop of 243 Medium battery and be a part of the medium gunners in support of operation of 23 Mountain Division. Thus, by December 6, 24 Medium Regiment with Regimental Headquarters, 27(Poonch) and 243 Medium Batteries, was deployed together as a Regiment and 26 (Murree) Medium battery was in support of 8 Mountain Division, opposite Sylhet Sector. 28 Medium Battery of 40 Medium Regiment was in support of 57 Mountain Division.

The original tactical plan, at the beginning of the war which was to contain the Lalmai defences, was changed, and 23 Mountain Division was tasked to contain the Lalmai Height's defences, Maynamati defences and also Laksham, and push a brigade through the gaps, to secure Chandpur. 61 Mountain Brigade of 57 Mountain Division which had 23 Mountain Regiment (75/24 mm guns) in direct support was tasked to secure the Northern flank of the division. The plan of advance was (See Map 5):

(a) 83 Mountain Brigade with 57 Mountain Regiment, in direct support to advance, along Axis Chauddagram-Parikot-Laksham.

(b) 301 Mountain Brigade under command 1 (Independent) Armoured Squadron with 197 Mountain Regiment, in direct support to operate further North, along main axis Nirbhayapur-Bhagma-Buschi and Leknagar-Mian Bazar-Kashinagar-Buschi. The Brigade, Divisional Headquarters and artillery brigade were to use Axis Kalikrishnagar-Buschi. This axis, according to the engineers, had no capability to take sustained vehicular traffic without extensive engineering effort.

(c) 181 Mountain Brigade with 198 Mountain Regiment in direct support to operate further north along approach Dhanpur-Bhagmara-Mudaffarnagar.

(d) The three batteries of 183 Light Regiment, had been grouped with different mountain regiments as Sierra (S) or Tango (T) batteries. Commanding Officer 183 Light Regiment, Lieutenant Colonel SD Khullar was the Divisional Deployment Officer for artillery regiments of the artillery brigade. Lieutenant Colonel Ashish Banerjee, Commanding Officer 24 Medium Regiment, organised an adhoc Counter-Bombardment Organisation, with elements of 124 Divisional Locating battery and Survey Troop of the Headquarters 23 Artillery Brigade, assisted by Captain KC Sharma of 24 Medium Regiment.

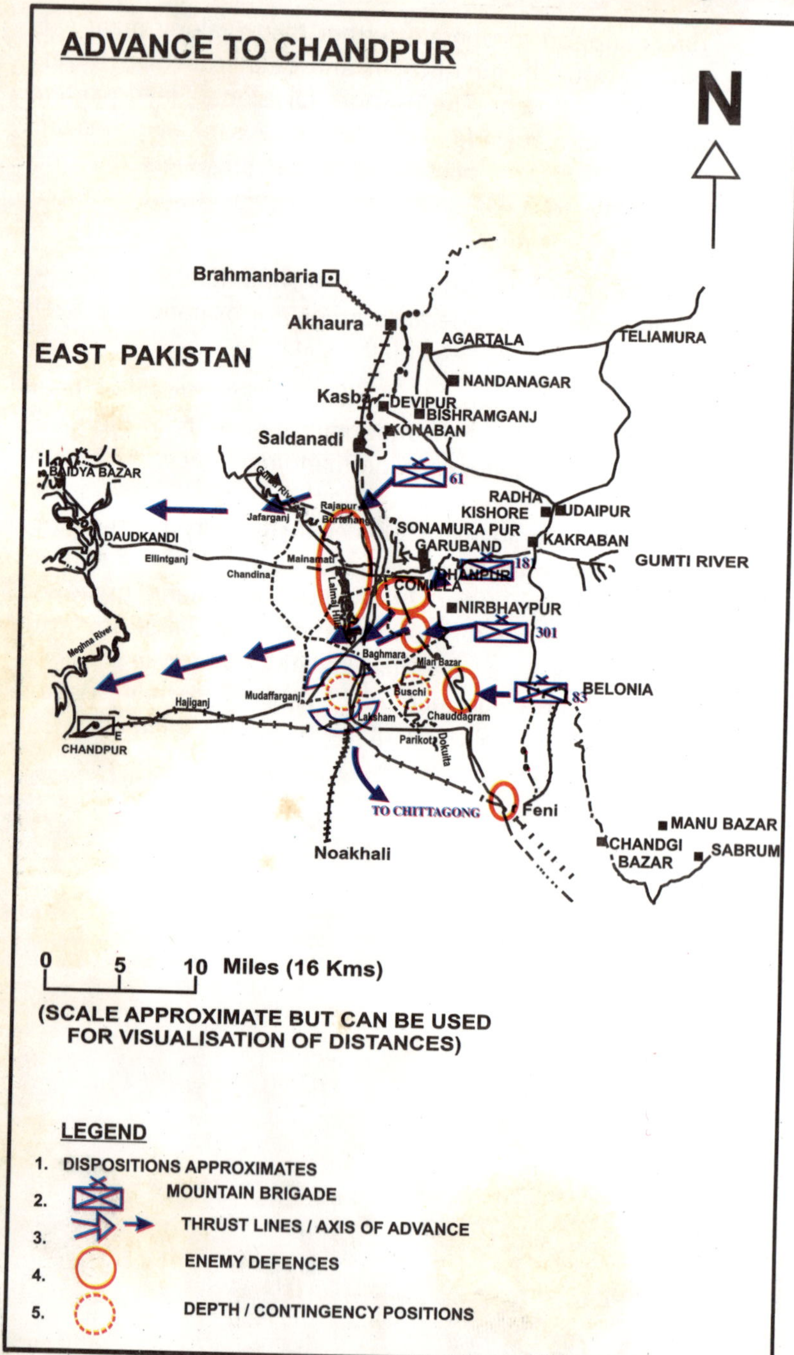
ADVANCE TO CHANDPUR
N
EAST PAKISTAN
Brahmanbaria
Akhaura
AGARTALA
TELIAMURA
NANDANAGAR
Kasba
DEVIPUR
BISHRAMGANJ
KONABAN
Saldanadi
61
BAIDYA BAZAR
Jafarganj
Rajapur
RADHA KISHORE
UDAIPUR
SONAMURA PUR
GARUBAND
KAKRABAN
DAUDKANDI
Ellintganj
Mainamati
Chandina
GUMTI RIVER
181
COMILLA
NIRBHAYPUR
301
Meghna River
Baghmara
Mian Bazar
Mudaffarganj
Buschi
BELONIA
83
Hajiganj
Laksham
Chauddagram
CHANDPUR
Parikot
Dokuita
TO CHITTAGONG
Feni
MANU BAZAR
CHANDGI BAZAR
SABRUM
Noakhali
0 5 10 Miles (16 Kms)
(SCALE APPROXIMATE BUT CAN BE USED FOR VISUALISATION OF DISTANCES)
LEGEND
1. DISPOSITIONS APPROXIMATES
2. MOUNTAIN BRIGADE
3. THRUST LINES / AXIS OF ADVANCE
4. ENEMY DEFENCES
5. DEPTH / CONTINGENCY POSITIONS

December 3-4, 1971 : The Commencement of the General War

301 Mountain Brigade commenced advance by infiltration of battalion groups of 14 JAT, 1/11 GR and 3 KUMAON (Rifles) on foot to depth positions, on evening and night of December 3/4,1971. First to open up was D Troop and later C Troop joined in, and a total of 40 rounds were fired. For the first time, during a lull in firing, I found that a detachment from the Electrical and Mechanical Engineers (EME) had come right up to the gun to weld and repair the gun, in the gun position itself—such forward repairs were a great morale booster and my senior command post staff informed me that, in war, one always gets the services coming forward rather than the user going back for repairs, as is the practice and procedures during peace.

Major. MC Ramanand, our Battery Commander as Link Sign 41 with 1 (Independent) Armoured Squadron, crossed the border, on early morning of December 4, 1971, and overcame opposition at Mian Bazar in conjunction with the Infantry of 301 Mountain Brigade and D Troop fired 30 rounds and by evening of December 4, 1971, 25 Frontier Force Battalion of Pakistan surrendered to our troops at Mian Bazar by then on December 4, the battery had fired 78 rounds. Thereafter, the advance was rapid with leading Observation Post Officers reporting crossing various control points (Charlie Papa)—three figure digits which were given to important landmarks like villages and towns. Soon, the medium guns were out of range, from the existing position, which can be referred as gun area Alpha (A) (See Map 6).

THE MEDIUM GUN AREAS : ADVANCE UPTO CHANDPUR

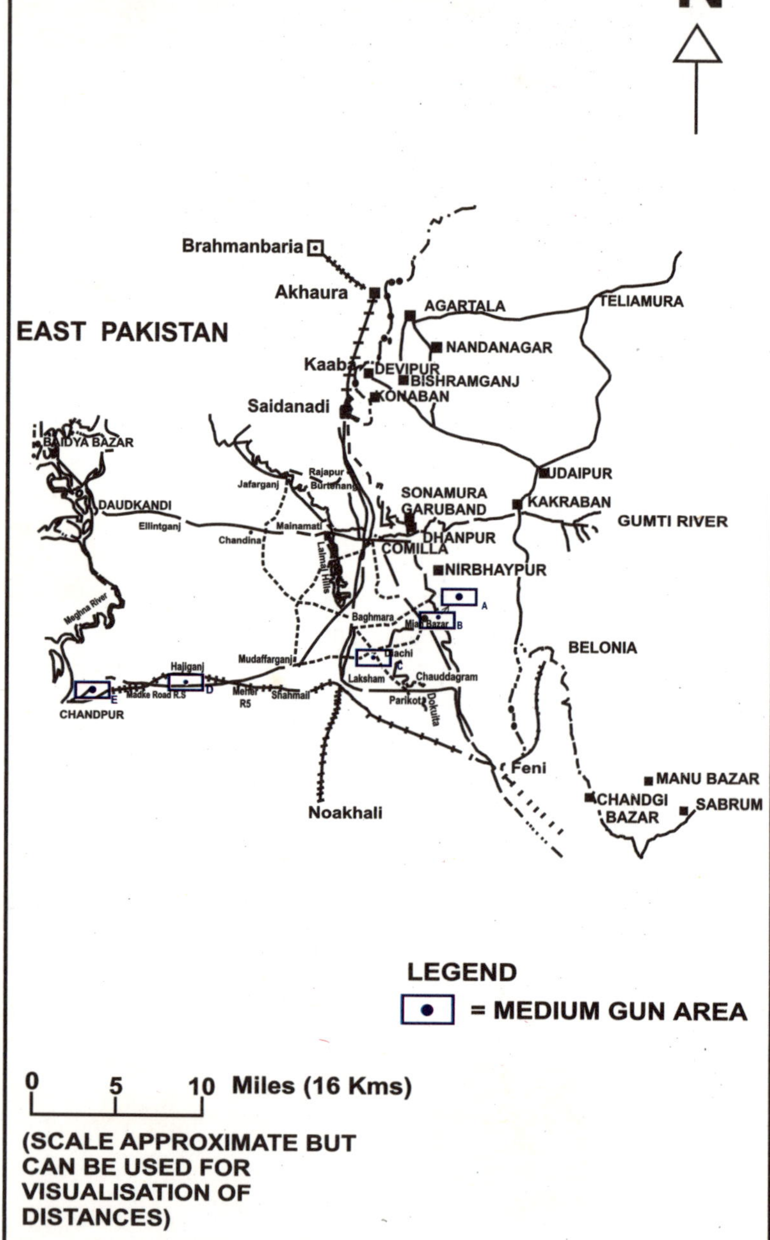

By 6 pm (1800 hours) on the evening of December 4, 1971, the guns of 27(Poonch) Medium battery, crossed into East-Pakistan, and deployed at Mian Bazar, 4 kilometres inside at gun area Bravo (B). By this time, 83 Mountain Brigade had commenced isolation of Laksham, by establishing various blocks. Captain RC Wolfe, as Link Sign 55, commenced engaging targets on the approaches to strong point of Laksham.

December 5, 1971

Early in the morning, elements of 301 Mountain Brigade, advanced towards Buschi, while 181 Mountain Brigade passed through 301 Mountain Brigade, without getting involved in heavy fighting, near the border, and successfully commenced isolation of Laksham, in conjunction with 83 Mountain Brigade which overcame Chauddagram defences, where 23 PUNJAB of Pakistan was badly mauled. The siege of Laksham had commenced and Pakistani troops of 53 Brigade withdrew and fell back on Laksham, during the night.

December 6, 1971

The situation now was that 23 Mountain Division had succeeded in penetrating through the gap of defences of Pakistani 117 Brigade, between Lalmai Hills to the north, and Laksham in the south. Also, the Southern thrust by 83 Mountain Brigade had been successful, and remnants of Pakistani troops of 53 Brigade, which were responsible for the southern approach, had fallen back and occupied the defences at Laksham. The siege of Laksham had commenced, as it was surrounded by Indian 83 and 181 Mountain Brigades. To further press on, it was decided to continue with the advance, with 301 Mountain Brigade on axis Mudaffarganj-Hajiganj-Chandpur, leaving the job of isolation ana containment of Laksham to 83 and 181 Mountain Brigade and that of Maynamati Complex to 61 Mountain Brigade.

The medium guns of 27(Poonch) Medium battery were getting out of range from gun area Bravo 'B' near Mian Bazar, the next deployment was ordered at Buschi (gun area 'C'), a distance of 30 kilometres. Now, as has been explained, although the engineers had done a marvellous job in improving the *kachha* tracks, there was heavy movement of vehicle columns and as we had gained total air supremacy, we were literally moving head to tail. The Krazes could negotiate and overtake road blocks by driving around the road blocks and traffic jams. As we approached Buschi, we could see tall pillars of smoke from Laksham defences probably some ammunition or fuel was on fire. The divisional artillery was also in the process of deploying in and around Buschi which had a small forest, ideally suited for administrative areas for the echelons. Enemy 105 mm guns were very active from Laksham defences and their artillery observation posts must have had a grandstand view of the Buschi corridor, which was dominated by observation from Lalmai Heights, through which vehicular column of 23 Mountain Division were now passing at slow speed.

It was a first regimental day-light deployment, as second troop from 243 Field battery had fetched up, after supporting the battle of Zakiganj, from 8 Mountain Division Sector. The gun area was on a junction of two *kachha* tracks.

As soon as the Reconnaissance Parties under Major Iqbal Singh Loomba, the Second-in-Command, and the Gun Position Officers reached the gun area, Charlie (C), Pakistan Artillery commenced shelling, which was fortunately very high airbursts and ineffective. Some rounds burst on the ground, but as the ground was very soft, no worthwhile splinters could hit any of the guns or crew, which came into action using quick action procedures. It appeared that it was unobserved fire of harassing nature, because of its inaccuracies both in the height of burst and closeness to the guns. December 6, 1971, was indeed an important day for the Pakistani 39 Division. Its 25 Frontier Force had already surrendered at Mian Bazar and 23 PUNJAB had withdrawn to Laksham, thus, leaving a wide gap on the Chandpur Axis in between the strong positions of Maynamati and Laksham. Laksham had now been built up with 15 and 39 BALUCH, together with two companies of 21 *Azad Kashmir* and its Headquarters. The General Officer Commanding 39 Pakistan Division, drove out towards Laksham from Chandpur, but had to beat a hasty retreat, when his party came under fire

from leading troops of 301 Mountain Brigade, ju
of Muzaffarganj.

The General Officer Commanding of 23 Mou
Major General RD Hira, who was moving up ne
had a charmed escape from Pakistani gunners but "the Wagon Lines of 183 Light Regiment and 'A' Echelons of 1 (Independent) Armoured Squadron, located at Buschi forest, together with a troop of 243 Medium Battery, were shelled by Pakistani gunners, and soon the ammunition caught fire and started exploding. Lieutenant Colonel SD Khurana, the Commanding Officer of 183 Light Regiment, with Subedar Major Sumer Singh of 183 Light Regiment, who was the Divisional Deployment Officer, attempted to control the situation but were killed due to exploding ammunition. The ammunition of troop 243 Medium battery, also caught fire, and Subedar Ran Singh and Havaldar Gurbax Singh showed presence of mind and exemplary courage in controlling the fire, thus saving the guns and ammunition. Havaldar Gurbax Singh was awarded the Sena Medal for his valour.[1]

It was noon and the guns of 27 (Poonch) Medium battery had since deployed and the air observation posts were engaging the enemy defences and guns at Laksham, when the above incident took place. The information at that point of time was sketchy and we got the news in bits and pieces from Sikh troops of 'A' echelon of 1 (Independent) Armoured Squadron who had escaped the explosions, which had taken place in their ammunition vehicles and had reached our gun position for safety.

The Pakistan gunners again fired a few high air bursts on the gun position and one could hear the falling splinters, fortunately no one was hit. The fire in the Wagon Lines had created a traffic jam on the main axis as the Army Service Corps drivers, while attempting to get away from the exploding ammunition, had blocked the road by getting stuck on the berms of the *kachha* track. To add further confusion, as we were busy engaging targets, when two persons in civil clothes, on cycles, who crossed us near the track of gun area, spread the alarm that an attack was developing from the south. This was a false alarm, and before we could nab them, they had disappeared. Probably, it was some jitter tactics experimented by the Pakistani defenders. On December 6, in the afternoon, a convoy of Army Service Corps trucks also called second line vehicles, under an elderly looking Major who reached the gun position with ammunition for the guns. It was yet another practical lesson in logistics, where ammunition to gunners is delivered forward at the place required, on a 'Push System' basis. It was a welcome sight to see such services under adverse conditions.

Our Air Force became very active, and although we knew that we had gained mastery of the skies, as a second nature when the first air attack came on Laksham, most of us took cover and dived; probably due to experiences of 1965 war, when maximum casualties had been caused by air attacks on the guns. The same night, we also heard the report of single barrel rocket launchers being fired on Laksham. This too, was a new battle noise and it took some time before we realised what had fired. The roar of rockets was impressive.® This adhoc unit of 262 Single Barrel Rocket Launchers (Grad-P) were raised post-haste and full credit must be given to its personnel for getting into grips with this new equipment of the Indian Army, under battle conditions. Similarly

® According to Lieutenant General JFR Jacob, in his book *Surrender at Dacca* (see Bibliography), in November, 12 Single Barrel Rocket Launchers (Grad-P) were formed in two batteries, one each with 23 and 9 Divisions. 9 Infantry Division could not employ these, as no rockets were available. Therefore, here at Buschi, for the first time, the Indian artillery employed rockets. Later, after the war, on getting back to 5 Mountain Division sector, the Grad P were issued as sector stores, and we all did short cadres, including its move on mule pack on mules artillery of 83 Light (Pack) Regiment. This was around 1973 or so. Later, during my familiarisation trip to the Siachen Glacier, in 1988, I spent two days at the helicopter maintained post at Amar, in the Northern Glacier with troops of 14 Garhwal Rifles. Captain Bharatendu Sharma, the post commander and me, resorted to using the Grad-P which had been converted to sector stores, to be operated by the infantry. The two rockets did perform well on Pakistani "three pimple" target but due to bizarre high altitude ballistic conditions, I doubt, they hit the target. Later, during the Kargil war, in 1999, for the first time, 122 mm multiple rocket launchers were used and even shown by the media.

in the western front we learnt after the war, that the 160 mm Heavy Mortars had been procured post haste from Israel. In war one always needs to be ready to absorb new equipment which also includes operating captured enemy guns, as was done by the Mountain Regiments with the captured Pakistani 105 mm later.

As concerns digging down for safety and security, no gun pits could be dug as the water table was extremely shallow and about a foot deep, instead, we resorted to *Sangars* or parapets to protect the guns. Subedar Faqir Singh recalled that such *Sangars* had to be constructed with stones. The battery was deployed in North West Frontier Province at Razmak before the Partition of 1947. Now, it was alluvial mud and earth, that was being used for constructing the same.

December 7, 1971

By December 7, troops of 301 Mountain Brigade had advanced further West, towards Chandpur, and Laksham had been contained by 83 and 181 Mountain Brigades. In support of the advance, the reconnaissance party moved forward to deploy at the next gun area Delta (D) at Hajiganj. As the enemy had blown up a bridge the gun group caught up with the reconnaissance party and was deployed temporarily, and fired a few rounds at the bypassed fortifications of Lalmai Hills, where 61 Mountain Brigade was exerting pressure and 14 JAT of 301 Mountain Brigade had been switched back to capture Comilla town and airfield.

December 8, 1971: Open Action near Hajiganj

By 1100 hours (11 a.m.), the battery had moved forward and deployed in general area Hajiganj (gun area Delta or D). The advance had been very swift and even from this gun area, the guns were out of range, as the enemy had withdrawn to Chandpur, an important town on the eastern bank of the mighty Meghna River, just 40 kilometres south of Dacca (See Sketch 2). At 1130 hours, Captain Rupinder Singh Brar,[2] the Observation Post Officer of 183 Light Regiment, operating with 2 RAJPUT, road protection group, caught sight of an enemy battalion strength, approaching the gun area about 2000 yards away,

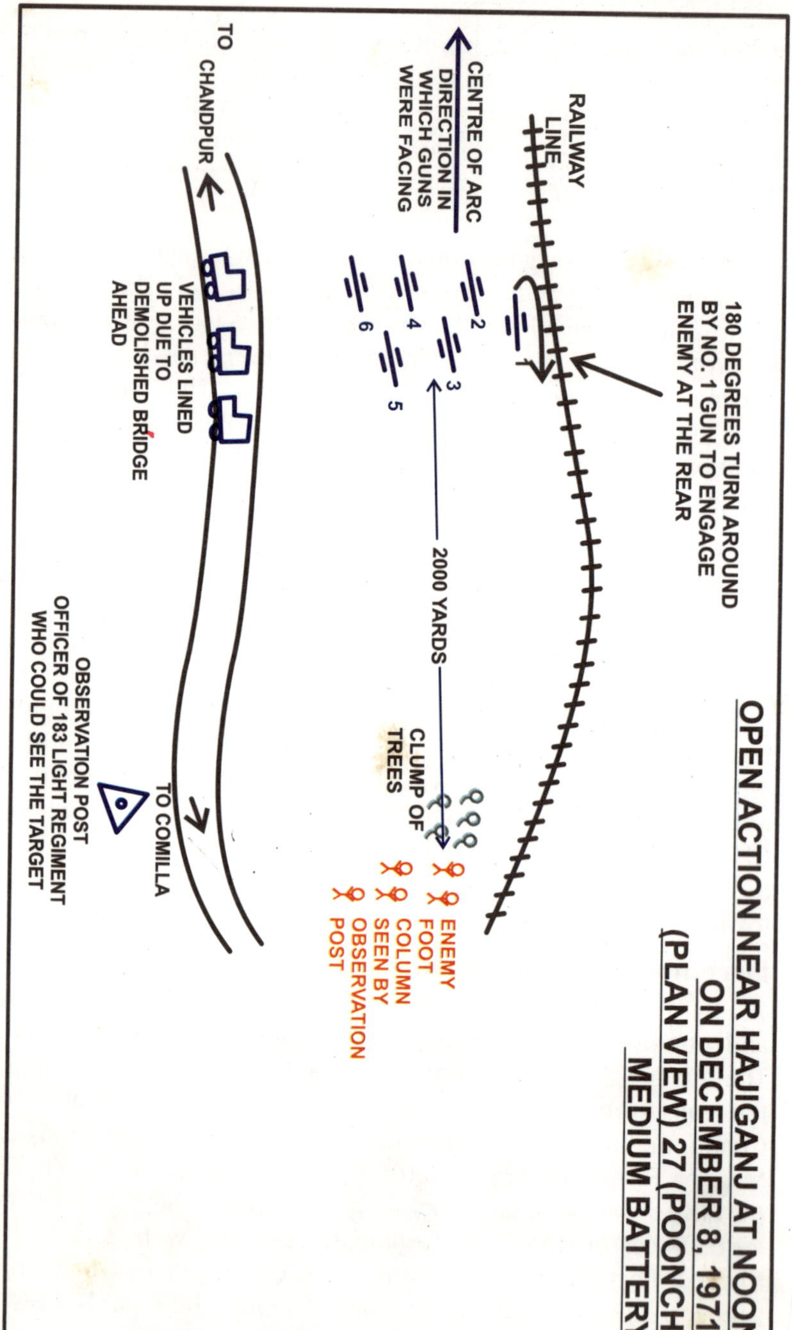
OPEN ACTION NEAR HAJIGANJ AT NOON ON DECEMBER 8, 1971, (PLAN VIEW) 27 (POONCH) MEDIUM BATTERY
RAILWAY LINE
180 DEGREES TURN AROUND BY NO. 1 GUN TO ENGAGE ENEMY AT THE REAR
CENTRE OF ARC DIRECTION IN WHICH GUNS WERE FACING
2
3
4
5
6
2000 YARDS
CLUMP OF TREES
ENEMY FOOT COLUMN SEEN BY OBSERVATION POST
TO CHANDPUR
VEHICLES LINED UP DUE TO DEMOLISHED BRIDGE AHEAD
TO COMILLA
OBSERVATION POST OFFICER OF 183 LIGHT REGIMENT WHO COULD SEE THE TARGET

and behind the gun position. He passed his fire orders on radio, and on receiving the fire orders, it was realised that, the target was behind the gun position, though not visible from the guns. C3 gun of Havaldar Mohinder Singh- 90 was turned around by 180 degrees and 32 rounds were fired, including airbursts. Later, *Mukti Bahini* picked up 19 dead bodies, 4 mortars and a vast quantity of arms and ammunition.[3]

A similar open action had been executed by the battery against the Japanese in Burma, in 1944, in the famous battle of 'Admin Box', where, the battery turned the tide of the Japanese offensive by holding out and protecting the administrative base, and Headquarters of 7 Indian Division. Of course, the action in World War II was on a much ferocious scale, and lasted many days. Annexure to Appendix A, has these actions of the Second World War recorded.

December 9-11, 1971

Chandpur had been secured by the leading troops of 301 Mountain Brigade, and Laksham had been abandoned by the enemy. The reconnaissance party moved up for the final gun area, Echo 'E', to support beyond Chandpur. Captain JS Jodha of Regimental Headquarters attached with the battery, while on the move with the guns and took the surrender of 120 Officers and men, including the Commanding Officer of 23 PUNJAB, who approached the gun group column. The Pakistan Army column thought it better to surrender to the Indian Army and be treated as Prisoners of War, rather than get captured by the *Mukti Bahini* and face dire consequences, as the heat of the revenge and memories of their crackdown must have been fresh in the minds of the *Mukti Bahini* forces. As the gun group was dashing forward to come into action, the prisoners were immediately handed over to 2 RAJPUT of 83 Mountain Brigade.*

* The history of the Regiment of Artillery *God of War* records that, "On December 10, 27 Medium battery of 24 Medium Regiment delivered another body blow to the enemy's morale by capturing the CO, Second in Command, a JCO and 49 other ranks (ORs) of 23 Punjab".

The guns reached gun area Echo (E) at Chandpur, which had been abandoned by the enemy. Three rounds were fired on an enemy steamship, on the River Meghna, and the target promptly hoisted a white flag and the Pakistani troops surrendered to 1/11 CR, though we learnt that as the ship came ashore, some jittery recruits of the Pakistan Army opened fire and caused casualties to the infantry, which was ready to receive the prisoners and a Khukri charge perforce had to be executed.

It was then the first lull in battle for the medium gunners but soon we got orders to swing back to action and provide fire support at Maynamati complex to 181 and 61 Mountain Brigades where the remnants of Laksham and troops of Pakistan 117 Brigade were holding out in their 'fortress' defence. Meanwhile, 301 Mountain Brigade pressed on towards Dacca, as a different and of course a spectacular manoeuvre phase of operations of IV Corps, using helicopters and all improvised means with formations such as 57 Mountain Division and 101 Communication Zone. We, the heavy and road bound artillery in turn raced back to Comilla and Maynamati cantonments for some set piece battles of attrition.

December 12, 1971

The battery moved back towards Comilla and deployed near Lalmai Railway Station for the capture of Maynamati defences. Throughout the move, nuisance mines had been cordoned off and were in the process of being removed by the engineers. The approach roads and tracks had since been improved by the Herculean efforts of our sappers. Meanwhile, after the fall of Laksham, 83 Mountain Brigade had been ordered to move south to Chittagong.

December 13 to 16, 1971

From December 13 to 16, the battery continued to engage targets in the Maynamati complex and the Battery Commander with 1 (Independent) Armoured Squadron had many occasions to ask for fire on enemy defences. As a static type of situation had developed, the sound ranging equipment of 124 Divisional Locating battery had deployed its base and the battery engaged enemy guns using sound adjustment techniques. The fluid nature of the tactical situation had since stabilised. 301 Mountain Brigade, with 197 Mountain Regiment, had advanced towards Dacca via Daudkandi. 83 Mountain Brigade had moved south, to join up with Kilo force, in their advance to Chittagong, shedding Captain RC Wolfe who had joined up with the battery after a frantic search, in commandeered civil hired transport. Captain RS Sandhu, after being an Observation Post Officer with 1/11 Gorkha Rifles of 301 Mountain Brigade, till the securing of Chandpur, had now been attached with 9 KUMAON of 181 Mountain Brigade, as 301 Mountain Brigade had moved out of area of our operations to Daudkandi, and to its West, for the race to Dacca. The reduction of Maynamati was the task of 181 Mountain Brigade, consisting of 6 JAT, 14 KUMAON and 9 KUMAON and 61 Mountain Brigade, consisting of 12 KUMAON, 7 RAJPUTANA RIFLES and 2 JAT, with 198 and 23 Mountain Regiments, in direct support. 1 (Independent) Armoured Squadron came directly under divisional control. Major MC Ramanand, as a Medium battery Commander, with his Driver Operator Gurcharan Singh, had operated throughout the operations, with armour either in a Jeep or Jonga or rode piggy back on the tank, as there were no tanks for the battery Commander's party. The battery Commander's party had been exposed to enemy fire throughout, and for keeping the radio communications through, Driver Operator Gurcharan Singh was Mentioned-in-Despatches. The gun position of 24 Medium Regiment had 27 (Poonch) and 243 Medium Batteries, deployed as a Regiment, and after a gap of nearly five months, both the batteries were next to each other. Various battle incidences and experiences were exchanged during the lulls in firing. We found that now, operating under fading war conditions, peace time comforts of the Mess were available and we had our first meal in the field Officers' Mess, which was set up near an abandoned school building. Our battery, on its own, operated without a mess, and for the first time, I met the non-combatant enrolled mess staff, who narrated great tales of war, as they had seen it in the Regimental Headquarters location, first at the concentration area at Kakraban in Tripura, and later near

Maynamati. As these non-combatant persons were not authorised personal weapons those days, I agreed to their lament that in war such as this, they must get rifles issued. The Adjutant, Captain BCS Jagati had also set up his Command Post in the gun area and one day, on the radio net, there was interception and intrusions by Pakistani radio operators, and we heard choicest and rustic exchange of Punjabi abuses by our Jat Sikh operators. The Pakistani intruders were no less in their linguistic knowledge, such was the experience of this 'electronic warfare'.

Our air observation post was very active. On December 15, it engaged enemy guns and tanks. One tank (Chaffe) was hit directly by C2 gun of Havaldar Kehar Singh. Later, the same gun also hit one gun of Pakistani Artillery. The guns then redeployed from kilometre-stone 7 on Chandpur-Comilla axis at kilometre-stone 5, short of Comilla. On December 16, in the early hours the battery engaged counter bombardment targets and the air observation post was successful in scoring a direct hit on an enemy gun with our battery. Attacks by 181 and 61 Mountain Brigades were launched and finally, on 1015 hours, on December 16, 1971, the enemy surrendered and cease-fire was declared. The air observation post helicopters thereafter, circled and dipped over the guns, as a salute, and flew away for tasks other than shooting sorties.

During the surrender ceremony, Brigadier Atif, the seniormost Brigadier of the Pakistan Army, and Commander of 117 Brigade, inquired as to who was Link Sign 41 on the radio (meaning the battery Commander, 27 (Poonch) Medium battery). He congratulated Lieutenant Colonel Ashish Banerjee, the Commanding Officer of 24 Medium Regiment, for the 'good shooting' done by the Regiment on them. Brigadier Shiekh Mansoor Hussain Atif further revealed that, as early as October and November, they had plans to raid or ambush the medium guns of 24 Medium Regiment, which were a cause of great concern to them. The location and movements of the medium guns were known to them, fairly accurately, but somehow they could not get to organise the mission, due to the threat of *Mukti Bahini,* in the countryside, which restricted their free movement.

Now, such appreciation by an enemy commander speaks volumes of the sportsmanship quality which Brigadier Shiekh Mansoor Hussain Atif had displayed in no small measure. *

When the cease-fire was declared, the battery had one gun loaded. The gun was moved to Lalmai small arms ranges and as a safety measure, the entire area was cleared off and the gun fired point-blank on the butt, using a remote lanyard as the firing lever. Thus, the last round was fired in very different circumstances, the battery having fired 2706 rounds earlier. We also saw the maps on a smaller scale, to see where all we had operated. We found a school atlas, which had the entire area of Agartala, Belonia and Chandpur on a small scale. This gave us a fresh insight from a vantage point. The school atlas had also the Tropic of Cancer marked with a dotted line, and we realised that all through, we were operating along the Tropic of Cancer!

End Notes

1. There were some reports that the Pakistan Observation Post Officer was decorated for the targets he engaged on December 6, 1971, in and around Laksham and Buschi. However, no published literature to confirm this, is available, which came to my notice during the research for this book. There was a general admiration for Pakistani OP officers, who were known to be daring and unconventional. Probably they also carry the same impression about us.
2. Captain Rupinder Singh Brar later joined the Cavalry, and won a gold medal in tent-pegging, during the 1982 Asian Games, at New Delhi. This event of Open action at Hajiganj was also published in the *Royal Artillery Journal* of UK, in its Autumn 2002 issue. For incorrect claims on this event, by some other unit and incorrect recording of military history, refer to *God of War* at bibliography.
3. Lachman Singh, Maj Gen, *Victory in Bangladesh,* Natraj Publishers, 1981, p.212. Rafiqui Islam, BU, *Tales of Million*

---

* He, being the Olympic Captain of the Pakistan Hockey team (for the interest of sportsmen, Appendix F may be referred).

Bangladesh Liberation War 1971/ Anna, 38/2 Banglabazar, Dhaka, 1995, Revised. p. 347. Salik Siddiq, *Witness to Surrender,* Oxford University Press, 1997, pp.176-179. Salik Siddiq, perhaps has given the most detailed account of the two columns which came out of Laksham, on the night of December 7/8, 1971, and till they finally surrendered to Indian troops by December 10, 1971, (inclusive probably of the column which surrendered to 27(Poonch) Medium battery). Lachman Singh has mentioned that these were columns comprising elements of 23 PUNJAB and 21 Azad Kashmir, moving towards Hajiganj from Laksham defences, when they bumped into the medium battery position. According to Rafiqul Islam, two fighting columns, under two Lieutenant Colonels, with troops of 15 BALUCH, 23 PUNJAB and 21 Azad Kashmir were tasked to clear Indian road blocks at Muzaffarganj. In 1999, a book by Colonel Brian Clougley, *A History of Pakistan Army* was published by Oxford University Press. The author, at page 214, quotes:

"The garrison of Laksham was surrounded by 181 and 301 Mountain Brigades but managed to make a clean break on December 7. Two groups were organised: one composed of the remnants of 21 AK and 23 Punjab, and the other, of two companies of 15 Baluch. They were intended to clear the enemy from Muzaffarganj, where 39 Baluch was besieged. They failed. 15 Baluch was ordered back to Laksham and the other column to Hajiganj, only twelve miles from Chandpur. 21 AK and 23 Punjab had a nightmare march, splitting up, and were both captured on December 10."

Appendix A

A Brief History of 24 Mountain Regiment

9 (Murree) Mountain battery was raised at Abbotabad, on March 1, 1898, followed by 12 (Poonch), which was raised at Dehradun on September 1,1907. These pack mountain artillery batteries operated independently at times, and under the need of re-organisation, came under Headquarters 24 Mountain Regiment, having served under different Headquarters. For example, 12 (Poonch) and 9 (Murree) were part of the following Headquarters, during the Second World War:

Regiment	1939-40	1941	1942	1943	1944	1945
21	9	9				
23	12					
24					12	12
27		12	12	12		
29			9		9	9

Note :-

Headquarters 24 Mountain Regiment was raised in 1932 at Abbotabad.

The batteries had two sections of 4 guns each, one section of Sikhs and the other Punjabi Musalmans (PMs). According to the *Hand Book of Indian Army on Punjabi Musalmans* written by Colonel JM Wikeley, Revised Edition, 1927, the four main divisions of PMs were Rajputs, Jats, Gujjars and Foreign Tribes. In September 1944, orders were received and the PMs were to be transferred to 21st Indian Light Mountain Regiment, which may now be the 1st Mountain Regiment with Pakistan artillery, consisting of 1st (Jacob's), 2nd (Kohat) and 4th (Lahore) Mountain Batteries.

At Partition, 24 Mountain Regiment consisted of:

2nd (Derajat) Mountain battery (Frontier Force) (Now part of 22 Mountain / Field Regiment), 9th (Murree) and 12th (Poonch) Mountain Batteries. 9th (Murree) and 12th (Poonch) were redesignated as 26 (Murree) and 27 (Poonch) Mountain Batteries. Both these batteries had participated in the First World War in Egypt and Palestine, and during the inter-war periods, and after World War II, in North West Frontier Province. 26 (Murree), immediately after raising, had sent one section for operations in East-Africa, at the end of 19th century.

During the World War II, both the batteries saw action in the jungles of Burma, against the Japanese. 12th (Poonch) Mountain battery had the distinction of having participated in the monumental withdrawal across the Sittang Bridge, and the Sikh section having the unique honour of bringing back the mountain guns intact. This was later followed by operations in the Arakans and the famous battle of 'Admin Box'. Later, the battery moved to Kohima, and finally took part in the advance and pursuit for the liberation of Burma. During this period, both batteries earned four Military Crosses, viz, Lieutenant Iqbal Singh, Subedar Fateh Singh, Jamadars Kartar Singh and Babu Singh. This is not a mean achievement, as a figure of four, out of the total of 11 awardees, from India (less UK and Pakistan), is more than one-third of the awards earned by the Indian artillery. Why was no Honour Title awarded, was hypothesized by me, in an article which was published in the *Artillery Journal,* of 1988. The same is reproduced as Annexure to this Appendix. Later, as has been mentioned in Note 1, to Chapter I, the *Royal*

Artillery Journal from UK, in its September 1996 issue (Volume CXXIII No.2), featured articles by participants in Burma. One such response was a Letter to the Editor, which was published with replies from the author of the article, Lieutenant Colonel R McCiag, MC, and a letter from him is also included in the Annexure to Appendix A.

The guns, though not the mules, varied from 2.5", 10 pounder B.L, 2.75", 3.7" and 4.5" Howitzer (How). Soon after independence, the regiment was converted to a medium regiment with 5.5" medium guns from UK, with the Mack as the gun towing vehicle, shedding the 3.7 inch pack Howitzers and the Mules artillery, and with it, the aura and charm of the pack Mountain gunner, eulogised in the famous poem "Screw-Guns" by Rudyard Kipling, thus:

Smokin' my pipe on the mountings, sniffin' the mornin' cool,

I walk in my old brown gaiters along o' my old brown mule,

Lieutenant Colonel (Later Brigadier) SS Kalha was the first Indian Commanding Officer. 27 (Poonch) Medium battery participated in the first Republic Day Parade, on 26th January, 1950, at the National Stadium, New Delhi. In 1961, the Regiment participated in 'Operation Vijay', in Goa, against the Portuguese. In the 1965 Indo-Pak War, the Regiment took part, usually divided and sub-alloted as batteries and sections, as part of 1 Corps Artillery Brigade, in the Sialkot sector, in 'Operation Nepal'.

In 1966, the Regiment was re-organised in the Sialkot Sector, into three medium batteries each, equipped with six guns. The third battery which was designated as 243 Medium battery, was raised on January 26, 1966, at Sialkot, West Pakistan, in the 'captured territory' of Pakistan (which was later vacated by Indians, after the 'Tashkent Agreement' in 1966).

A Special Note on the Murree Battery

Background

On March 1, 1899, 9th (Native) Mountain battery was raised at Abbotabad, which is now part of divided India (Pakistan). Thus, another battery was added to the Indian mountain artillery. The fascinating birth and growth of mountain artillery needs recalling a bit of Indian history. Regular artillery companies had been approved by the East India Company in 1748 for the three Presidency Armies of Bengal, Madras and Bombay. With the conclusion of Second Sikh War, the British were faced with the untamable and wild North-West Frontier stretching to some seven hundred miles of rugged mountains, from Hazara to Sind. Mountain artillery came into prominence on this account. Thus, before the Great War of Independence (called 'Great Indian Mutiny of 1857', by the British), the artillery of the Company consisted of mountain units, the horse artillery and foot artillery (Field gunners). The last two were made of British and Indians, but the new mountain trains consisted of Indians only under a British commanding officer. The war of independence saw almost the entire Bengal native artillery rise in arms, except the newly raised mountain trains and the Horse field batteries employed on the Frontier. In 1858-59, the British did away with Native artillery. The European part of India's artillery was handed over to Royal Artillery. Two mountain trains, the three Punjab Irregular Force (Piffer) batteries and two Bombay Native artillery companies were to survive, plus four field batteries of the Hyderabad contingent. The Piffers became the 1st (Kohat) Mountain battery Frontier Force (FF) and 2nd (Derajat) Mountain battery FF, whilst the Peshawar Mountain battery became 3rd, and Hazara, the 4th. At the same time, the two Bombay batteries were renumbered as 1st and 2nd Bombay Mountain Batteries. The 1st Bombay battery of 57 Mountain Regiment, with unbroken service since 1827 thus, became the 'Oldest Indian unit of artillery and with effect from 1990, Indian artillery celebrated 163 years of history, on 28 September, every year, as the 'gunners' day. Thitherto, the 1935 date of raising of the 1st Indian Field Brigade, had been 'Observed as the raising day (15 January).

The four Frontier Force batteries and 2nd (Bombay) were engaged in the Second Afghan War, whilst Hazara battery and the 1st (Bombay) went on to Burma for service, in which two additional mountain batteries were raised, 7th (Bengal) at Rawalpindi and 8th (Lahore) at Mian Mir. The 1st and 2nd (Bombay) were re-numbered as the 5th and 6th, respectively. After the Punjab Frontier Campaign of 1897-98, the 9th (Murree) was raised at Abbotabad in 1899 and the 10th (Abbotabad) in 1900-01. Thereafter, in the 20th century, suffice to say, further raisings were ordered and numbering and renumbering was done before, during, and after both the World Wars. The 9th (Native) Mountain Battery became the Murree Mountain Battery in 1901; 29th Mountain Battery, 1903; 29th Pack Battery, 1920; 109 (Murree) Pack Battery, 1921; 9th (Murree) Mountain Battery, 1927; present designation being 26 (Murree) Medium Battery (SP).

The Animals, Equipment and Men

To the old pack mountain gunners, it was the rustic charm of animals, equipment and men, or soldiering was an equation of animal, equipment and man management. 9th (Murree) Mountain battery was raised with 2.5" howitzer, which had to be transported or moved on mules. On raising, the battery had 4 ponies and 76 mules. The mule artillery (MA) or *Khachar* is a cross between a donkey-stallion and a pony-mare. It inherits its hind portion from a horse and the fore portion from a donkey. This inheritance makes it a very tough, sturdy and sure-footed animal. The Driver Mule Artillery (DMA), for some strange reason, always suffered privation and miseries, which no other soldier in the army has had to suffer, but, the heady mixture of mountains, howitzers and mules was too overpowering for any worldly comforts. Therefore, the stoic mountain gunner has an elan of his own.

Murree battery was raised with a mixture of Jat Sikhs from the Punjab and the Punjabi Mussalmans (PMs), into separate sections. After the partition of India, the battery had only Jat Sikhs. The guns and howitzers with Murree battery, makes interesting reading, as the Table below indicates:

Guns Used by Murree battery

Year	Equipment
1898-99	2.5″ RML (SCREW GUN)
1903	10 lb B.L
1918	2.75″ inch B.L
1919	3.75″ How
1921	2.75″ B.L
1924	3.7″ How
1945	4.5″ How
1949	5.5″ BL (Medium gun)
1974	130 mm M 46 (Medium gun)
1981 onwards	130 mm M 46 Catapult (Self Propelled)

Active Operations

Murree Mountain battery has had a chequered operational career, as the diary of operations indicates.

Diary of Operations

Serial Number	Operation	Date	Sector	Remarks
1	Jubaland Field Force	December 24, 1900 - July 2, 1901	Jubaland, Africa	First Mountain battery of the Indian Army to be deployed in Africa
2	Miran Shah	January-April 1915	Tochi Valley North-West Frontier Province (NWFP)	

3.	Egyptian Expenditionary Force	May 1918-June 1921	Middle East	
4	Razmak Column	December 1924 - February 1926	Razmak, NWFP	
5	Bajaur Mohmand	August - September 1933	NWFP	
6	Khajuri Force Afghan Blockade	October 1939 - May 1940	NWFP	
7	South East Asia Command (SEAC), XIV Army	December 1942 - October 1944	Burma	
8	Tribal Action	January-May 1946	Wana, NWFP	
9	Operation Vijay	December 1961 - Jan. 1962	Goa	
10	Operation Ablaze	May-August 1965	Maldibari, Islampur	
11	Operation Nepal	September 3-23, 1965	Sialkot	
12	Operation Cactus Lily	December 1971	Bangladesh	
13	Operation Rakshak	Early 1990s	Punjab	Counter Insurgency
14	Operation Parakram	December 2001 - October 2002	In concentration and staging areas for war with Pakistan	Not a shooting war but mobilisation carried out as a strategy of coercive diplomacy

Subedars Subil and Shadam Singh were awarded the Order of the British (OBI) 1st and 2nd class respectively, in June 1941, and Lieutenant Iqbal Singh was awarded the Military Cross (MC) in 1944, in the Campaign in Burma, against the tough Japanese. Iqbal Singh was for a long time attached as a Forward Observation Officer (FOO) with 1/4GR.

Independent Nature of the Mountain Batteries and their Further Renumbering

The Indian mountain artillery batteries operated independently, most of the times. For the need of re-organisation, Murree battery served under different Regimental Headquarters, during the Burma Campaign, in World War II, as under:

1939-40	1941	1942	1943	1944	1945
21	21	29	29	29	29

9th (Murree) and 12th (Poonch) were renumbered as 26 (Murree) and 27 (Poonch) Mountain Batteries. As the Table of equipment shows, soon the Regiment converted to Medium Regiment with 5.5" BL, and thereafter to 130 mm M46 (Towed). In line with the traditional elan of mountain artillery, the Murree battery is now a Self-Propelled or SP battery, or a part of 'Horse Artillery'. It has been more than a 100 years of warfare, from Pack to 'Horse Artillery', from mountain and jungle warfare to mechanized manoeuvre warfare; from mules to computers of the Information Technology age in the nuclear era. To preserve their independent nature under the secure Regimental Headquarters (RHQ), Murree battery (like all mountain batteries) still proudly updates its battery history book, which is in manuscript form. The historian is generally the erudite 'Gun Position Officer and the Editor the Battery Commander himself.

Post-Independence Operations

In 1961, 26 (Murree) Medium battery participated in 'Operation Vijay', in Goa, against the Portuguese. In the 1965 Indo-Pakistan War, the battery deployed in sections or independently as part of 1 Corps Artillery Brigade in the Sialkot

Sector. The battery equipped with 5.5" gun gave a telling account of itself and maintained fire supremacy for the depth and contact battle of the manoeuver arm. After the 1965 war, the batteries were reorgnised from eight guns (two sections) to six guns each. 243 Medium battery became the youngest and the third battery of 24 Medium Regiment in 1966.

When the 1971 Indo-Pak War was to break out, the battery was deployed under 5 Mountain Division on the Sino-Indian border, in the Sela sector of North-East Frontier Agency (NEFA), now called Arunachal Pradesh. During November 1971, as a part of strategic decision making by the highest headquarters, the battery with five guns was de-inducted from NEFA and moved down south, to the borders of erstwhile East-Pakistan, in support of 8 Mountain Division, which was the northern pincer of IV Corps, opposite the Sylhet sector. During the swift campaign, the battery being the only medium battery in the division, was in popular demand, and it lived up to its reputation by sustained mobility in the marshy and boggy terrain of Bangladesh, delivering the 80 pounds shell of 5.5" gun, on targets. One troop was taken across water obstacles in engineer rafts and was even towed by a 3 ton 'Shaktiman' vehicle, the balance of 'Horse Power' being provided by the 'heave' of the gallant gunners of Murree battery. Successful conclusion of operation by 8 Mountain Division was very much a function of mobility, quick response and accurate firepower by the Murree battery. All this while, one lone gun, under a No. 1 (the Commander of the gun, in the rank of a Havaldar) maintained vigil in the snow-covered Himalayas, to repulse a Chinese attack (which never materialised).

Since mid-1970s, as a part of 24 Medium Regiment (SP), with sister batteries, 27(Poonch) and 243 Medium, the battery was converted to the self-propelled role and though still having the traditional and inherited passion of pack artillery, the battery is the pivot of fire-power of the armoured formations. It measures victory with fire power, thanks to the gallant animals, the superb officers, Junior Commissioned Officers and the *Jawans.* 'CHABBIS BATTERY' is the role model of the Indian artillery more than one hundred years have proved it !

Sources Referred for Appendix A and Further Reading

1. Battery History (manuscript) of 26 Murree and 27 Poonch Batteries, extracted to the author by the unit-24 Medium Regiment (SP).

2. Colonel HCB Rogers, *Artillery Through the Ages,* (London: Seeley Sercice & Co., 1971).

3. John, Gaylor, *Sons of John Company: The India and Pakistan Armies 1903-1991',* (New Delhi: Lancer International, 1992).

4. CHT MacFetridge and JP Warren, *Tales of the Mountain Gunners,* (Edinburg: William Blackwood, 1973).

5. Brigadier General CAL Graham, *The History of the Indian Mountain Artillery,* (Aldershot: Gale & Golden Ltd, 1957).

6. Charles Chenevix Trench, *The Indian Army and King's Enemies 1900* - 1947, (London: Thames and Hudson, 1988).

7. *Outline History of the Regiment of Artillery,* Artillery Institute Press, Deolali.

8. *History of the Indian Artillery; Indian Army,* (New Delhi: The Directorate of Artillery, Army Headquarters, 1971).

Annexure to Appendix A

(Refer to Endnote 1, Chapter 1, p.81 and Appendix A, pp.88-89)

Copy of an Article Titled 'The Unclaimed Honour Title of 12 (Poonch) Mountain battery', Published as 'The Unsung Valour of a Mountain Battery, written by the author and published in the 'Artillery Journal' 1988.

Introduction

The pen is indeed mightier than the sword. From a study of recent Indian military history, it becomes evident that we have not given due attention and care to war diaries, regimental and unit histories, despatches, war accounts, biographies and memoirs. In spite of being burdened with tremendous amount of paper work, historically speaking, we have not recorded our acts of bravery and courage in its totality. A timely citation or claim for a battle honour or honour title is first and foremost a matter of the pen. Many units have been lucky in having officers who could write, immediately on occurrence, various citations and diaries and, of course, the clerks to produce the typed version. Many units unfortunately, had a wonderful set of officers, who were so involved in the day-to-day operations, that it never occurred to them to pen down the various deeds of valour, except to fight, attend to the mules, care for the men and equipment and beat the enemy at any cost. This article deals with the war accounts of 12 (Poonch) Mountain battery, which is now called 27 (Poonch) Medium battery, forming Part of 24 Medium Regiment (Self Propelled).

The Withdrawal from Burma

To briefly recapitulate, the Japanese attacked 'Burma' in 1942. The British had the 17 Infantry Division, and later, during the withdrawal, 1st Burma Corps was formed, consisting of I Burma Division, 17 Infantry Division, and 7 Armoured Brigade.

Various accounts of the battles in Burma have been analysed, from different points of view, to highlight the honourable deeds of 12 (poonch) Mountain battery, that deserved distinction and yet, went unnoticed.

Maj Gen Shelford Bidwell, in his book *"Gunners at War"*:

General Bidwell is a retired Gunner Officer of the British Army. He has to his credit a number of books, articles and essays. His account can be summarised as :

"The gunners of I Burma Corps, can boast of a fighting retreat of 700 miles, perhaps 1000, as they marched, from Moulmein in lower Burma, to Imphal in Manipur, lasting five months, and crossing four great rivers, the Salween, the Sittang, the Irrawady, and finally, the Chindwin. All that remained of the 150 pieces of artillery of the Corps, were ten 25 pounders, eleven 3.7 inch howitzers and four 2 pounders which, after tremendous exertion, were brought back to India. The survivors were cheered by their Corps Commander's laconic greeting, "Good", said Lieutenant General Slim. "You've still got your guns with you"! (Page 204).

Brigadier General CAL Graham, in his book, " *The History of the Indian Mountain Artillery* " :

Brigadier General Graham, has vividly biographed and recorded, in the minutest details, the exploits of 12 (Poonch) Mountain battery. For the benefit of our young readers, it can be recounted that, the battery comprised, a Sikh Section, and a Punjabi Musalman (PM) Section. Various excerpts from the book are given below :

*Sittang Bridge Disaster, February 1942**

"Sikh Section of 12 (Poonch) battery was the leading artillery unit and Lt JOS Janson decided to cross, as soon as he could. The bridge being blocked with transport, he unloaded the mules and loaded guns and ammunition on a steamer, the vessel was hit and set alight by enemy fire, just as it reached the opposite bank, but the guns were saved by the detachments, who carried them up-beach and came into action, keeping a steady fire to cover the crossing". (Page 311).

Further withdrawal due North, March-April 1942

"The Sikh Section of 12 (Poonch) Mountain battery never failed in its support of the Infantry, occupying one defensive position after another; always in pack, its longest march was for forty-one miles, followed as usual by digging on arrival. No men fell out". (Page 314).

"The Sikh Section of 12 (Poonch) Mountain battery was still marching and fighting during its latest withdrawal; it recorded a march of eighty seven miles, by night and day, with nothing more than tea for sustenance." (Page 317).

"The 12 (Poonch) battery was in action with 17 Infantry Division and contributed to the clearance of Japs (Japanese), and safe-crossing of the column. Both sections, now complete, the Punjabi Musalman Section having joined up with its guns. During the action, this section was again forced to destroy its guns, but the Sikhs followed through with the division and brought the last two mountain guns over the Chindwin. Of the twenty five guns, saved in the corps, eleven were 3.7 inch howitzers" (Page 318).

"The Sikh Section of 12 (Poonch) Mountain battery earned Corps Commander's congratulations".

---

* The British forces were trapped on the enemy's side of the bridge. The bridge had to be blown and troops on the far bank had to swim across to the near bank. A number of casualties took place. The PM Section was forced to destroy its guns here. Later, they were rearmed with new guns in the withdrawal.

The book *"History of the Indian Artillery"*

The book has not dealt with the operations of individual units or sub-units. It has however, recorded the battle of Sittang and the number of guns saved, thus:

"12 Mountain battery supported 17 Infantry Division at the battle of Sittang" (Page 73).

"Out of 104 guns, just four 25 pounders were brought back to India". (Page 77)*

Extracts from Battery History Book of 12 (Poonch) Mountain Battery

The battery history book contains manuscript accounts of the 'Burma' Campaign. In all old units, battery history is the most authentic document. Quoted below are extracts from the book:

- "January 1942- The Japs attack Moulmein from the south, and the first round is fired by Punjabi Musalman (PM) Section, in support of 5 Burma Rifles".
- "11 to 16 Feb 1942- The Japs attack, and having managed to infiltrate or turn our flanks, we move back to prepare another defensive line, and the same sequence of events takes place. During this time, there was never any real reserve, and the troops are continuously in the Frontline".
- "22 Feb 1942- HQ Sikh Section cross Sittang river at 0620 hours to take up position, to support 11/4GR ... PM Section is caught at Moulmein and quite heavy fighting ensues, wireless communication closes down between the three brigades involved".
- "23 Feb 1942- The Sittang bridge is blown, leaving the two brigades".
- "March 1942- Both sections rejoin Pegu, where personnel are re-equipped".
- "March 1942- Sikh Section marches to Tokyan, where 17 Division is held up by a strongly defended road block,

---

* No mention has been made of the 3.7 inch howitzers brought back by the Sikh Section of 12 (Poonch) Mountain battery in this book. Even Gen. Bidwell, quoted earlier, has acknowledged that eleven 3.7 inch howitzers were brought back. Brigadier General CAL Graham also mentions eleven 3.7 inch howitzers.

perfectly sited ... a two battalion attack is put in. Sikh Section suffers three casualties from bombing".

- "April 01, 1942- The Japs attack the position (at Prome) by bayonets at 2000 hours. An hour later, the road block is over, the guns are successfully withdrawn, with only a few minutes to spare, and move out of PROME".
- "April 2-8- Series of long marches back to Taungdwingy".
- "April 8-19- Sikh Section moves to Tizang and then back to Yeyu, where news is received that Burma Army is withdrawing to India, via Tamu-Palel route. At Sweyoin, a force of the Japs block the crossing, and both sections come into action, fighting continuing during the day. PM section fires off their ammunition on a pre-arranged barrage and their guns and lorries are destroyed. Both sections (Sikh with guns) move with 17 Division by a back-route, and cross the river at Kalewa".
- "May 16- Arrival TAMU after marching up the Chindwin Valley".
- "May 18- PM Section moves back to Imphal. Sikh Section moves as rear guard to 17 Division, arriving at Imphal, on 23 via Lockchaw and Palel. This section were the last mountain guns to come out of 'Burma' and the battery was the first to be in action when the Jap aggression on 'Burma' took place ..... During the campaign, the battery fought and marched a distance of 1200 and 8 during a period of three months."*

Withdrawal from Burma, was indeed the first step towards "Defeat into Victory", as has been borne out by Field Marshal Slim. 12 (Poonch) Mountain battery, therefore, truly and honestly deserves the honour title, 'Burma 1942'. The deeds and acts of bravery are:

- The Sikh Section never lost their honoured 3.7 inch Howitzers to the Japs, throughout the withdrawal.
- The battery marched 1208 miles during a period of three months.

---

* The battery history book confirms the previous accounts by Bidwell and Graham. The Sikh Section brought its mountain guns intact.

- The battery was the first to be in action against Japs in Burma and the guns of Sikh Section were the last Mountain guns to come out of Burma.
- The brilliantly executed withdrawal operation of war, undertaken by Slim, was always supported at the rear guard by the gallant gunners of 12 (Poonch) Mountain battery.

The Battle of the Admin Box

Consequent to the withdrawal in 1942, the battery, after rest and refit, was moved to Arakan, under 39 Infantry Division, in 1943, and later came under the command of 26 Infantry Division. In the second half of 1943, it formed part of 7 Infantry Division.

Operation in 1944

The 14 Army had now been formed. In February 1944, the Army consisted of 15 Corps in Arakan, and IV Corps in the Imphal Kohima area. The Japs had a master plan called, "March to Delhi". Their plans were, firstly to destroy 15 Corps in Arakan, and thereafter, launch the main effort to capture Imphal plains. The Japs plan was based on the time proven tactics of establishing blocks in the rear. It was a decisive moment when the Japs struck 7 Infantry Division first, at Arakan. The 7 Infantry Division HQ was overrun, the remains of the HQ fell back to the divisional administrative area, called the Admin Box', at Sinzewya, near the Ngakyedauk Pass. It can now be recalled that, defeat of the Japs in the battle, was the turning point in the entire history of the war. The Japs were defeated for the first time, and this victory in Arakan, acted as a catalyst for further victories. This victory hinged on the famous battle of the Admin Box', which students of military history have studied with awe and reverence. It was again the gallant gunners of 12 (Poonch) Mountain battery, who stood fast, blasting their guns at point-blank range, at the charging Japs, over open in sights in the moonlit and dark nights of the Arakans in 1944.

The accounts given by various sources are now illustrated:

Shelford Bidwell in *"Gunners at War"*

Gen. Slim's orders were that, in the event of a formation or unit being cut off, it was to stand fast and fight, while his reserves first checked the infiltrators, and then, in co-operation with the troops in position, destroy them.

One of the more notable feats of arms that arose from this policy, is known as the 'Battle of the Admin Box', or the Sinzewya Box, or officially as the 'Battle of the Ngakyedauk Pass'. The correct name for an 'Admin Box' is the 'Divisional Maintenance Centre'.

5 and 17 Indian Divisions were disposed on either side of Ngakyedauk Pass and were well placed for a defensive battle, or for the offensive, that General Slim was about to launch.

The brigade boxes were so placed as to permit the artillery in each, to support the other. The storm centre of the battle was the Admin Box, and the smaller box, about three miles away, in which Headquarters of 7th Division, organised for defence against a raid or patrol, but nothing stronger. The 'Admin Box' was also organised for defence, this being in the hands of headquarters, and the light anti-aircraft batteries of the 24th Regiment, and various oddments.

The Japanese, realising that an offensive against them was imminent, planned, what was really a spoiling attack.

Early in the morning of February 1944, the Japs surprised the divisional headquarters, and attempted to storm it. Position became desperate, and the headquarters breaking small parties into it, moved back to the 'Admin Box'. Next day, Command Personnel of Div HQ had concentrated at the 'Admin Box'.

The artillery order of battle in the box was :

C Arty
HQ and two batteries 24 LM Regiment (L 60)
Bty 5.5" guns 6 Med Regt.
2 x Indian Mountain Batteries, 11th (Dehradun) and 12th (Poonch)
Mortar battery of 139 Regiment
Adhoc mortar bty.
Gunner infantry company organised on cooks, tradesmen and AA gunners.

The population of the maintenance centre, was under continuous artillery and mortar fire and repeated attacks.

When they (Japs) charged the perimeter, they were broken up by heavy fire, the howitzers (Mountain Artillery) firing point-blank. Eventually, after 16 days, the 'Admin Box' was quite unsubdued, and the 55th Jap Division was caught between the three Indian Divisions, and experienced their first crushing defeat and a severe moral shock. The Royal Artillery and its Indian Comrades can look back on the 'Battle of Admin Box' with pride, and claim a share in the victory, as great as any". (Page 211 onwards).

Brig. Gen. CAL Graham in *"The History of the Indian Mountain Artillery"*

"HQ 7 Division was overrun at the dawn of 6th, and fell back to 'Admin Box', where PM Sec of 12 Bty was there. The Sikh Section of 12 (P) fought its way through an ambush, with great determination to reach the Box, and had suffered some casualties, before settling into a small box on the edge of the main 'Admin Box'. The enemy cut the Ngakyedauk Pass on 7 Feb.

On the night 7/8 Feb hospital in Admin Box' overrun- own mountain guns fired in many directions, at point-blank range. On 10th all-night attacks were beaten back. The Sikh Section of 12 (P) was withdrawn under fire to rejoin batteries in 'Admin Box', after three days fighting. Lt Bagshawe and Jem Kartar Singh were awarded the MC for gallantry, driver Hav Mukund Singh of 12 (P) was awarded Military Medal for outstanding leadership.

A gun of 12th battery, received a direct hit by 75 mm shell, but was in action again the same day". (Pages 343-344).

The Book '*History of Indian Artillery*'

The Japanese launched their famous offensive in the Arakan early in 1944. 5, 7 and 26 Indian Infantry Divisions held out in the Arakan, the Japanese attacks being blunted by the famous boxes formed by 7 Indian Infantry Division, 7 Indian Field Regiment and 24 Indian Mountain Regiment participated in these battles. They then supported 5 Indian Infantry Division to relieve hard pressed 7 Division. Jemadar Kartar Singh was awarded MC at Ngakyedauk Pass. Hav Mukund Singh received Military Medal" (Page 77-78)*

Battery History Book - 12 *(Poonch) Mountain battery* (page 55 onwards)

"Considerable small arms firing was heard during the night to the North-East of the Position. The battery moved back again approximately 1500 yards. North-West moving by sections now tie up with 11 battery who are just behind Regiment Headquarters. Forming a self-contained box. Rumours and report of Jap infiltrators are strong. Foremost gun opened up on an enemy party moving nonchalantly down the road towards the gun Position.

The Sikh Section, under Lt. Manohar Singh, moved back to the Commanding Officer's position near the foot of the pass and were heavily mortared and machine gunned en-route, the casualties man - 1 wounded, mules - 3 wounded.

PM Section and 11 battery moved back a further 1000 yards, forming another 'Box' with B echelon of Yorks and 3/14. Position attacked from North and West unsuccessful.

"DF tasks selected DF 1 Range 425, DF 2 Range 600, DF 3 Range 3000**. Yorks bag 42 of the enemy on the South West of the box, a considerable amount of documents and maps were recovered. Capt Worthington killed".

"Message received from Churchill - I am watching your battles with intense interest. Remember what matters is the will".

"Message received from Mountbatten - Hold on and you will make history".

---

* The artillery order of battle as given earlier in Bidwell's book, has only mentioned two Indian mountain batteries, 11th (Dehradun) and 12th (Poonch). The book, *History of Indian Artillery* has mentioned in general and broad terms, the units of XV Corps. 12th (Poonch) battery, of 24 Medium Regiment, did not support 5 Infantry Division, to relieve 7 Division as is mentioned here.

** These are DFs selected at point-blank range. The laying obviously would have been direct.

"Watering of animals is rather difficult, as the water-point is continuously sniped. Tension considerable."

"Enemy shell landed in D Section gun pit on parapet. Casualties 1 killed,S wounded. Sights damaged. Within half an hour the gun was in action again".

"Night Attack - They (the enemy) infiltrated into the Sikh section wagon lines by 0600 hours. They have been driven back, leaving 31 bodies and a good quantity of equipment including a sword. Our casualties—personnel killed 2, horses 4 killed, 3 wounded; mules - 11 killed, 13 wounded. A party of *japs* heard coming over the Ridge, engaged by guns and mortars, shouts indicate damage, reasonably quiet.

Ngakyedauk Pass opened after heavy fighting.

"Japs in small portions are withdrawing by whatever route they can, to Buthidang Road".

"No opposition met, the FOO closes down and returns to the battery".

From these accounts, it is now certain that, a major share of the fighting, during the epic battle of the 'Admin Box' was done by the gallant gunners of 12 (Poonch) Mountain battery. It appears paradoxical that the battery did not get the honour tittle 'Sinzewya' or 'Admin Box'. Obviously, as mentioned earlier, the pen was not given due importance. There can be nothing "time barred" when historical deeds of valours and gallantry are unearthed and researched in a fresh light and from a broader and wider viewpoint. The battery has earned the honour tittle 'Admin Box".

Remaining Parts of the Burma Campaign

After the Arakan battle, the battery was the first to move up with 161 Infantry Brigade for the relief of Kohima garrison. After the battle of Kohima, the battery took part in the general offensive, till finally Burma was reconquered.

Operations After Independence

For the benefit of readers, briefly the 1965 and 1971 wars are being summarised, as fought by the battery. In both wars, the battery displayed excellent performance.

- **1965 war** - The battery was now a medium battery and was equipped with 5.5 inch Howitzers. It participated in 'OP Nepal', in the Sialkot sector in September, 1965. Having supported the Battle of Akhnoor-Chamb, the battery moved out to Sialkot, and supported the Indian advance towards Phillora, in support of 43 Lorried Brigade. It was pivotal in beating back the famous counter-attack on Phillora, by Pakistan. Infantry units were later awarded the Battle Honour, 'Phillora'. 5/9 GR is a case in point. However, the battery's claim for Honour Title "Phillora", was probably never made, just as in the Burma Campaign.
- **1971 - Bangladesh** - The battery commenced operations from July 1971, till the final war in December 1971. It supported the entire 4 Corps Sector. It fired 2706 rounds and most of the rounds hit their targets. The battery was awarded a true "Honour" at the surrender ceremony at Comilla Cantonment when Brig. Atif the Commander of Pakistani Forces, complemented the unit by saying that, "It was the medium they feared most - good shooting 24".

In both the wars, no honour title was claimed, nevertheless, they had been earned.

Conclusion

12 (Poonch) Mountain battery, now 27 (Poonch) Medium battery (SP) of 24 Medium Regiment (SP), should truly be a recepient of honour title "Burma".

As stated earlier, the titles and honours were never claimed. It is not the object to get into wrangles and knots with the nightmarish procedure of claiming honour titles that are 45 years old. As long as our readers (both old and young alike) have read this story - the battery is convinced that the honour titles have been awarded - if not on paper then at least in the hearts of the readers.

LETTER TO THE EDITOR BY THE AUTHOR, WITH REPLY PUBLISHED IN THE 'ROYAL ARTILLERY JOURNAL,' AUTUMN 1997, NO.2, VOL. CXXIV, PAGES 60 TO 61

Gunners in the 'Admin Box'

from Colonel P K Gautam (Col GS EDP Enclave, India)

Dear Editor,

Please refer to the Journal of the *Royal Artillery,* September 1996, Volume CXXIII, No.2.

I had written an article on 12 (Poonch) battery of 24 Mountain Regiment, RIA in the *Artillery Journal* of 1988 which was published under the title 'The Unsung Valour of a Mountain battery', a photocopy is enclosed. I had referred to Brigadier General CAL Graham's seminal work, 'The history of the Indian Mountain Artillery' and also the battery history (maintained in manuscript, until today, in the original book) which had mentioned that the Sikh Section later rejoined the other elements in the 'Admin Box' and Lieutenant Bagshawe and Jem Kartar Singh were awarded the MC, and Driver Mukund Singh, the Military Medal..

In the article 'The Second World War—gunners in India, Half a Century Ago, Part 5', in your esteemed journal by Lt Colonel R McCaig MC, on page 20, at Serial 21, only one section is given in the order of battle, and at page 21, while explaining the air photo (serial 21 again), it has been mentioned in brackets that the Sikh Section had been involved in an ambush, 'possibly' with 3/14 Punjab, and never made it back to the main 'Box'.

May I request that this anomaly be further cross-checked as I am quite certain that the Sikh Section was very much in the fight. You can also refer to the book, *Tales of Mountain Gunners* edited by William Blackwood (Edinburgh) which has a chapter on '12 (Poonch) Indian Mountain battery in World War II', by AB Howard (page 138), where it is mentioned that, the 'Sikh Section successfully extricated ... '

I had also obtained a typed copy of the battery history, in mid-1980, and am enclosing photocopies of relevant typed pages (typographical errors are regretted).

Yours faithfully

P.K.Gautam

REPLY

From Lieutenant Colonel R McCaig, MC

Dear Sir

Colonel Gautam's letter from India of 3 January 1997 and the copy with it of his article published in their Artillery Journal on the 12th (Poonch) Mountain battery RIA, raises interesting matters concerning the time of this battery in the Arakan.

Firstly, in my article, referred to in the September 1996 issue of our Journal, the schedule of units in the Admin Box, on page 20, taken straight from the book *Golden Arrow,* is admittedly not wholly accurate. The position for 24th Mountain Regiment (item 21) is properly shown later, on page 21 of my article. My brief comment about the Sikh Section of 12 Bty. should not be read as meaning that they were not "very much in the fight"—undoubtedly they certainly were, but the Sections reportedly had become separated. (The Mountain Batteries, by their nature, often found themselves right up in the front line). The graphic accounts detailed by the Colonel of their actions then are dramatic, and moving.

Again, 24 Mtn Regt was, of course, part of the 5 Indian Divisional Artillery and such elements of theirs only really came under our control in 7th Indian Division when in the Admin Box.

It must be realised that, the whole of the Kalapanzin Valley had suddenly been set ablaze. Desperate fighting broke out everywhere and many ad hoc 'boxes' were initially formed, stoutly resisting the Japanese onslaught. Subsequently there was movement as the battle developed in succeeding days and weeks.

Quite recently I did have most interesting meetings with each of the two British officers mentioned by the Colonel, (respectively BC and GPO involved), and also with the author JP Mellors, *('Shots in the Dark'* 1974), the Signals Officer of 24 Mtn Regt then. They may be able to provide first hand information about the movements and actions of these batteries at this time. If the Colonel would wish it I could try to put them in touch.

I may say that I am very much in sympathy with the cause of this article mentioned above covering the outstanding record of 12 Bty throughout WW II, and subsequently. In earlier articles in my series now I had referred to the high quality and proud place, in action of this elite corps, the Mountain Gunners; and I had specifically highlighted the sterling performance of this battery in the long, valiant fighting retreat when we initially opposed the Japanese in Burma. Their battery Captain at the time has recently produced a very interesting paper on this : I must see if I can get a copy, or at least extracts from it, for the Colonel. They would interest him.

Yours faithfully

Richard McCaig

(one-time BMRA 7 Ind Div)

LETTER RECEIVED BY THE AUTHOR FROM LT COL R. McCAIG, IN RESPONSE TO THE LETTER WRITTEN TO THE EDITOR, 'ROYAL ARTILLERY' JOURNAL

Telephone: Newbury (01635) 43774

15, Gorselands, Andover Road
Newsbury, Berkshire, RG14 6PU, UK
11 Aug, 97

Colonel PK GAUTAM
PMO ACCCCS, EDP Enclave
Rao Tula Ram Marg
Delhi Cantt. - 11 0010, INDIA.

Dear Colonel,

12th (Poonch) Mountain Battery RIA

Your letter of 3 Jan'97, to the Editor, the Journal of the Royal Artillery about this battery has been received with much interest: it will draw a response.

Meantime I forward to you herewith a copy of the 5 page letter of 30 May'94, written to me by Major Elsworth, with his permission, that should add to your already very expensive knowledge of this fine battery's record, in WW II. It is his account, written at my request of the battery's fortunes in the first Burma Campaign. He was then the battery Captain, no doubt principally concerned with the maintenance, provisioning and supply, as well as deputy to the BC John Hume. (He has since moved to a new address in the UK).

John Hume was one of my greatest friends and he subsequently related to me at length his experiences in our first long encounter from India with the Japanese. He was in great spirits, and very proud of the performance throughout of his battery.

Sadly John did not survive the war, and I thought recently to see if Nigel Elsworth could let us have a record of what they had been through - hence, his letter now.

With best wishes,
Yours sincerely,
(Lt Col R McCaig)

LETTER WRITTEN IN 1994 BY MAJOR GNF ELSWORTH T.D THE BATTERY SECOND-IN-COMMAND (BK) OF 12 POONCH MOUNTAIN BATTERY, DURING THE FIRST 'BURMA' CAMPAIGN, WORLD WAR II, TO LIEUTENANT COLONEL RICHARD McCAIG, THE THEN BRIGADE MAJOR, ROYAL ARTILLERY, 7 INFANTRY DIVISION.

Major GNF Elsworth T.D.
0544 318944

Low Gables,
Ledgemoor,
Weobley,
Herefordshire,
HR4 8RL/

30th May 1994

Dear Colonel McCaig,

Thank you for your letter of 23 May. John George Learmouth Hume was about the finest and most pleasant officer that I ever served with. When not called John he was known by the other B.O.s in the Bty as, "The Gallant Leader" which he undoubtedly was. I joined 12 Bty in September 1941 from 5 Bty in Wana under Hugh Wilberforce.

In Moulmein the Bty lines were some miles from the town with the animals in a rubber plantation. When we came inside the perimeter all animals were withdrawn across the estuary to Martaban. John, with the PM Section, supported the 4/12 FFR on the South part of the ridge and the Sikh Section took up a position adjacent to the famous Kipling Pagoda further North. BHQ was in the American Mission School below the ridge. By road it was a long way from there to the guns but the Sikh section could be reached by a very steep path up the side of the ridge. I was with the Sikh section when they fired their first rounds at a steamer full of *Japs* coming up from the East with a large flying flag. This steamer was hit and beached and casualties must have been inflicted.

On orders to withdraw to the jetty I got the Sikh section there and then began to wreck the tpt and push some into the water. There was some trouble getting the PM section away. Miles Elton was slightly wounded and John had to collect some jawans from the 4/12th to recover the guns. We left Moulmein on the last steamer. Brig. Bourke, John Janson and I were lying on the deck and the *Japs* were firing at our departure. Then the firing stopped and the Brig, who knew all our Christian names, said to John Janson, "Are we now out of range of those guns?" John replied, "Definitely Sir". A few minutes later a shell landed 200 yds. short, but correct for line, and then another also on line but 200 yds. plus. The sarang rang all the bells for extra steam and hauled the wheel far over and the jawans began to take off their boots. I then realised that, we might well have to swim for it; an unwelcome thought. However and for reasons unknown, there was no fire for effect and the *Japs* allowed us to get to Martaban but gave us hell on arrival causing many Gurkha casualties. On arrival we realised that John was missing and we became worried. Later he arrived having been with a sapper called Ward in a motor-boat carrying out last minute demolitions.

The 24 hours prior to Sittang were about the worst I can remember. We were marching along a track inches deep in sand and the RAF, having been given the wrong bomb line, gave us all they had. Bombers and fighters at naught feet. Miles Elton and I had a personal bomb on my truck and we had to jump for it. Later, when marching across paddy fields the Bty was in double extended order and we were machine-gunned. It was surprising how few casualties we had but some mules had to be shot. When the planes came over the jawans lay down, dvrs. holding onto the lead reins and then got up again and marched on. I also saw the RAF L.O. at Div HQ, sitting in the bottom of a slip trench trying on the radio to get the RAF to stop firing, but in vain.

Later it was decided that the bty, less the PM section would support the advance guard 1/4 GR and the PM was ordered to another Bde. Why it was necessary to split a Mtn Bty when there were three other Btys there is something that I never found out. I joined the M.T. column in the late evening and John Janson marched the Sikh section to the river where he was to cross on the ferry. No animals were to cross on the bridge. Due to a lorry which became stuck on the bridge and could not be pushed over the side because of side girders, the column was delayed for hours and I did not approach it until about 0700 hrs when the *Jap* firing began. I think that the Bty's two trucks were about the last to get across and after finding a gun position in the paddy fields went to the jetty to meet the guns. They were shot at and received casualties some being fatal. John Hume was with Joe Lentaigne CO of 1/4 GR. Subedar Jawala Singh established an OP at the Westend of the bridge and our gun position was near Bde HQ. Thus when Gen Smyth and Punch Cowan (BGS) visited Bde about twice a day they always stood near us and generally in hearing distance. They came and spoke to us.

John was with 1/4th when the bridge was blown and I was in the gun position. I shall never forget the bang at about 0300 hrs. Later that day those on the far side started to swim across. They included 5, 15 & 28 Mtn Btys and our PM section with Miles Elton. I remember meeting John Lock of 15 Bty with whom I had served in Razmak and who was furious that he had lost and destroyed his guns. From this time, when all these gunners who had crossed were sent North to refit, we never saw or heard of our PM Section again. Miles Elton spent months in hospital and I can only assume that the jawans met up with us in Ambala after the campaign was over but I do not really know!

At Pegu we happened to be at the West side of the road block which the *Japs* erected and were then ordered to Taukkyan where the *Japs* had erected another block. I was met by my old Colonel from 25 Mtn in Razmak, who was now BRA, John Birbeck. He ordered me to get the guns into action in support of an attack on the block. Several attacks failed to break through and a final assault was ordered for the first light the next day, when the Bty supported 7th Hussars with signallers laying cable alongside the tanks. In the middle of this a Honay tank came through from the North and it was found that the *Japs* had flown leaving some snipers in the trees. These were knocked off and later the tpt started to move North. John Janson and I happened to be standing at the edge of the road by the block when General Alex and his ADC passed in an open Humber staff car. Alex had a small dog on his lap and the ADC a pistol. We saluted but both the General and his ADC looked directly in front completely ignoring us. John Janson of short temper exploded and castigated the General for not even giving us a slight wave of the hand. No doubt he was a very worried man but perhaps Monty would have reacted otherwise.

At Prome I found a gun position in the garden belonging to the Chief Forest Officer who, wearing a dinner jacket, was just leaving. He said to me "My wife is nursing in Maymyo and I am now to be attached to Div HQ for intelligence. The bungalow and all the contents are yours". He had just walked out. It was fully furnished in every way and plenty of tinned food etc. We stocked the mess with everything we wanted, I gave a large kerosene frig to the 7th Hussars who had masses of tpt and retained for myself a silver tankard and a coffee set with silver gilt holders such as we had at home. Alas, both these articles disappeared before we reached Shwegyin. The *Japs* attacked one night and we were lucky to get away without casualties. The OP was over-run and Jawala Singh and his signaller were jumped upon from behind. They undid their webbing and slipped their hands through and Jawala shot the *Japs* with his tommy gun. The guns had to make a hasty retreat down the side of a steep hill at the bottom of which an AT cart had overturned causing some delay. Come daylight and marching North there was no sign of Jawala or the signaller. We became very worried. Then from far behind a cyclist was spotted. It was Jawala on a female machine which he had found and the signaller was seated on the carrier. Never were we more relieved.

Now to Shwegyin. As I said earlier, the Bty was generally with the rearguard, and we thus arrived with 1/4 G.R., when most of the troops had already arrived and passed through. We supported the 1/4th on the Southside. The main *Jap* attack was from the West and the fighting became so mixed that only Charles's bofors could fire without hitting our own Inf, 1/7 G. R. and 1/9 Jats. Over open sights the bofors knocked out the *Jap* Mtn gun which was causing a bit of trouble. When the firing began the sarang of the steamer then loading at the jetty made attempts to get away but was dissuaded with a pistol to remain until fully loaded. The last steamer then departed leaving the only exit along a narrow track on the side of the river and then opposite Kalewa crossing by steamer. All tanks, MT and several guns were destroyed and the men then started along the track. Many were wearing thin shoes and were not used to marching. The very last troops to leave were 1/4 G. R. and 12 Mtn Bty (less PM Sec.) who fired a long barrage before leaving. John had said that we must leave ready to come into action again and all leather ammunition boxes were full and specialist equipment taken. I cannot remember how many mules we had but the mess was reduced to one or two yakdans and B.O's valises were allowed. I am not sure but I think that a mini bedroll for every 2 or 3 jawans went on top of the normal loads. It was late evening and the track was narrow. From time to time loads became stuck causing some delay. Next day we crossed to Kalewa by steamer and then marched in stages to Imphal. Although I would have been responsible for the admin *bandobust* I cannot remember how many days it took or anything about it. I marched at the rear of the Bty and the monsoon started causing my red and blue side hat which we often wore in 12 Bty to become very dilapidated. The jawans, of course, were still wearing their red fringes in their *pagris.* Nearing Imphal I like to think that John gave the order, "Eyes Front". It was the sort of thing he would do and with the jingle jangle of the harness and seeing these magnificent Sikhs with their heads held high who had marched every inch of the way from Moulmein, over 1000 miles, with guns which had opened fire by Kiplings Pagoda and the last to fire at Shwegyin, I became very proud that I had the opportunity of serving in such a Bty under John's gallant leadership. All the high standards came from him and Subedar Jawala Singh was an outstanding VCO. I cannot remember any cases of indiscipline or argument. All officers got on very well together. There was minimum sickness and although we were somewhat tired we were also pretty fit. I do believe that if we were able, after a few days rest, to march along the Silchar track and join the railway to Ambala, this could have been done. But no, John left us and we had to move to a ghastly camp at Kanglatongi, inches deep in mud, the monsoon in full swing and then sickness and reaction set in. Also, after being an independent Bty the whole time we were in Burma, it was not pleasing to come under an RHQ who we had not seen before.

Charles and I agree that only 18 guns reached India. 10 of these were Mtn guns, which were brought out on Bty mules. 8 x 25 pdrs. were got out from Shwegyin because the Essex Yeo requested and were given priority on the last steamer. It is not quite the same thing and this, I think, is what Anson Howard meant in his article.

We also believe that the photograph in Carmichael's book is of 23 Bty taken on arrival at Shwegyin. They did not stay there long and moved off along the track shortly after arrival. We believe that, the officer in bush hat and S.B. belt was the adjutant Brennan who often wore an S.B. belt. The bush hat was worn by the KOYLI from whom Brennan may have got one. Since Carmichael was in 23 Bty it could be usual for the photograph to be that of Bty.

I have been told on good authority that John was recommended for an M.C. by Brig Bourke but somehow in the retreat the citation became missing. A very great shame as fully deserved.

That is all I can remember about the tactical side but there are a few admin matters and the lighter side of the campaign. Most soldiers would agree that a mobile war is far more interesting than a static or semi-static one, and compared to what I experienced later in the Arakan, Tiddim and Bishenpur, the retreat from Moulmein was by far the most enjoyable and with scope for initiative. The atmosphere was more akin perhaps to the Desert Army under O'Connor. The weather was also far more to my liking.

Apart from 7 Arm Bde. who had masses of tpt and were able to carry around a piano, I reckon that 12 Mtn Bty enjoyed a pretty high standard of living. It began at Moulmein when a chinaman, Leon Chye, who owned the grocers stores decided to clear out North without locking the door. I managed to get there a short head of the Div. M.Ps who had arrived to ensure an equal distribution to the fighting troops. A and B mess in Div. HQ. Our private T model Ford Tourer was filled with goodies, there was everything from champagne to bath, oliver biscuits and the M.P. appeared to miss it because it was a private car. From then on I always cleaned my teeth from a bottle of Gordons Mixed Cocktail.

No vehicles were allowed on the last steamer to leave but I found a Norton motor cycle in a ditch and persuaded the Staff Captain, Jimmy Lunt, to get it aboard. It was a godsend at Martaban and later until forced to hand it over to the original owners. 4/12 FFR.

Outside, Pegu John warned me that there was a sort of "free for all" in Rangoon and the vet and I took his two horse ambulance to the bonded vaults under the Strand Hotel and loaded up with hooch. The limit was 100 cases per officer and including Dennis the vet and Jawala Singh I signed blind for 500 cases. Since all this would not go in the vehicle we arranged to come back the following day. It was then suggested that a change of clothing would be welcome and we were taken to a large store and given about 20 minutes to take away exactly what we wanted. The policeman with us stayed outside on guard. Unfortunately we could not return next day because the sappers were blowing the place up. Naturally the distribution of most of this drink within the Division made us very popular, and this also may have been the reason why we seemed to get, when not in action, so many visitors for a drink and natter. Without doubt, the most amusing and welcome of these was the CCRA, Brig. G de V Watchman and his BM Major R.J. Lloyd Price (ex 5 Bty) who seemed to come several times a week. The CCRA was a most charming man and kept us with news of what was happening elsewhere. Using all our Christian names he found the funny side of most incidents. The CRIASC, Brig Sammy Woods, was another friend of ours. He always said, "Is everything, all right? Can I get you any thing?" And then proceeded to tell us, what muddles other units had got into.

Tpt was now a problem, and the trucks were overloaded. Salvation came when John told me that extra vehicles were available from a Chinese lease lend dump near Taukkyan station from where I collected 2 Marmon Harrington armoured cars. They were in crates but 7 Arm Bde. fitters had charged the batteries and drilled out the ignition key holes. All we had to do was put on the wheels and drive away. A gun fitter was encouraged to drive and we were in business. One of the cars became my personal vehicle and made it to Shwegyin. Also about this time we acquired some fowl including a cock, which travelled in crates until needed for the pot. I also got from somewhere a monkey which was chained to the metal structure of the truck. This menagerie caused some comment and amusement from marching tps and I feel was good for morale. Unfortunately he disappeared later in the campaign as I should have liked to have got him to Imphal chained to the wheel and axle mule and watched the reaction of those already there. It might have even raised some mention in later articles about the campaign.

However, it was the opportunity to take further stocks from the Forest Bungalow in Prome which put us in the top division. Decent cutlery and crockery, napery and some chairs and a card table.

After Prome we were ordered to send back all our followers who were still with us. They were taken to a train which was stopped in a field near some depot but there was no station platform. With the followers was the Imprest Account chest under armed guard and some equipment. All got into the train and then the guards dismounted to help load some equipment. The train started to move and somebody shouted out the urdu for 'Shunting Sahib'. But, no, without stopping, it disappeared over the horizon, leaving the Imprest chest to be looked after by a *mochi.* Of course, it was never seen again and for months afterwards I was pestered by the FCMA in Poona to account for the loss or produce the missing cash. I am reminded here of an apocryphal story of the paymaster in Moulmein who, when fighting began and being doubtful if he would get away put all his cash in a rowing boat and rowed out in the estuary and dumped the cash overside. Got an MBE for conduct beyond the line of duty. Not true of course.

One other matter of note was my personal interview with the Corps Commander. Retreating every few days the MT went in a separate column from the marchers and there was always some delay. One day, everything stopped as usual and one waited in the vehicles until movement began again. We were all very tired and it was a common occurrence. Musing quietly to myself I found a face within inches of myself asking politely the cause of the halt. I said that I did not know and at the same time became aware that the voice was coming from a Lieutenant General - one Slim. The voice then became less polite and castigated me for being so idle as to do nothing. I was ordered to hasten at the double to the front and report back. Of course the trouble was that sepoy Ram Singh had just gone to sleep and the other drivers had done likewise. Awakening them the convoy proceeded and General Slim then reminded me again that officers should be alert at all times and not sit back and do nothing. A great and likeable man, perhaps the greatest General on our side in WW II.

Since starting this letter I now remember that on arrival at Imphal and before moving to Kanglatonbi I was asked by Brig. Sammy Woods, the CRIASC if I would like to join a small foraging party of officers to Calcutta to get comforts for all the Div Messes. I collected a shopping list for the Bty and was then told that I was to be responsible for obtaining all the drink. Relaxing in the Great Eastern Hotel was wonderful as was getting new uniforms from Rankins. Then I visited all the agents for the various brands, far more than there are today. Some sampling was generally offered and then as many cases as were prepared to sell, were ordered to be delivered to Sealdah station, on a certain date for loading with all other purchases into a sealed wagon, which was to be attached to our train. Trans-shipment was necessary from wide to narrow gauge and we also had to cross the Brahamaputra river by steamer but eventually we got everything to Imphal. I was very lucky indeed, to get this opportunity of visiting civilisation again and getting re-kitted before returning to the mud camp at Kanglatonbi.

I fear there is a lot of waffle in this but you may find some items of interest.

All best wishes,

Yours ever,

Nigel Elsworth

Appendix B

(Refer to Note 3, Chapter 1)

Brief Technical Characteristics of Ordnance Breach Loading 5.5 Inch Gun

1. Height at top of equilbrator	– 8 feet and 7 inches (These equilbrator springs look like a pair of horns)
2. Weight	– 114 cwt.
3. Length	– 24 feet and 8 inches
4. Ground clearance	– 1.75 feet
5. Width	– 8 feet and 4 inches
6. Barrel Construction	Loose barrel, auto frettaged, short jacket screw and shrunk, breaching and removable breech bush
7. Types of grooves	– PPS Uniform
8. Number of grooves	– 36
9. 1/20 calibre of twist	
10. Type pressure	– 70 pounds per square inch

11. **Recoil System**

(a) Recuperator	– Hydropneumatic annuls type
(b) Buffer	– Rotating valve
(c) Air in recuperator	– 800 pounds per square inch
(d) Oil in recuperator	– 28 pints
(e) Oil in buffer	– 18 points
(f) OIl in tank	– 6 pints

12. **Recoil**

(a) Metal to metal	– 55.85 inches
(b) At 0 degree elevation	– 54 inches
(c) At 45 degree elevation	– 30 inches

13. Trails. Split

14. **Barrel**

(a) Plan diametre	– 5.5 inches
(b) Length of rifling	– 135.32 inches
(c) Probable life in equivalent full charge (EFC)	– 4500
(d) Maximum number of rounds which may be fired between examination	– 1750
(e) Barrel rotation	– After 250 EFCs through 120 degrees
(f) Barrel inspection	– After 350 EFCs
(g) Quarter of life	
1st	– 5.500 to 5.558 inches
2nd	– 5.559 to 5.615 inches

3rd – 5.616 to 5.673 inches

4th – 5.674 to 5.730 inches

(h) Details of Guns with 27 (Poonch) Medium battery in 1971

Registration Number	Troop No	Quarter of Life	Last Calibration Done
L/2078	C1	First	March 1971
L/1833	C2	First	November 1963
L/1877	C3	Second	-do-
L/5844	D1	First	-do-
L/5613	D2	First	February 1962
L/2586	D3	First	November 1963

(i) **Ammunition:** 80 pounds high explosive shell fused with Direct Action Fuze 117 or time and percussion Air Burst fuze 213. Charges are bag loading from, one, two, three, four and super. There are no brass cartridges and the only residue, after a round is fired, is the smoke with a war-like and overpowering heady smell of cordite. The difference between a shell and a cartridge is surprisingly not well understood by many. Shell is often mixed up with cartridge. So, often many drawing rooms and even officers' messes have table lamps or tables with props or bar stools, made out of the brass cartridges of empty and used artillery cartridges, like the 130 mm gun, 25 pounder and 105 mm Indian Field Gun. The colloquial term for this is, "Shell". After taking part in the operations in Bangladesh, when the unit returned back to its location in NEFA, there was an increase in the infringement reports by the military police, against the most trivial reasons. On further inquiry, it was found that, the provost was expecting some 'Shells' to be presented to them, as war souvenirs, by an artillery unit just returning from war. On not finding any offer for this memento, the unit was placed under strict scrutiny, to express the displeasure. Later, an officer was made to visit the military police, and explain the nuances of not having any 'shells' to be presented.

(j) **The Digging Tool called *Kassi:*** The ordnance issue pick and shovels, were not very popular when the question of digging gun-pits for these guns arose. The handy digging tool, used all over Punjab by farmers, called *Kassi,* was the preferred choice. Anyone returning from leave, used to bring one, and it used to be paid out of regimental funds.

Some War Experiences of the Gun

5.5 inch Howitzer was the first medium gun of our Army, to enter service with Indian Artillery on independence. During the 1947-48 J&K Operations, this gun was broken up into separate parts and air-landed at Srinagar by 40 Medium Regiment. It was the only medium artillery in J&K with India and Pakistan. Pakistan's 8 Medium Regiment supported it in the Uri sector, at times firing the 100 lbs shell. This gun also participated in the liberation of Hyderabad in 1948, and Goa in 1961. It was used extensively in close and general support during the 1965 Indo-Pakistan War. Its sterling performance during the 1971 Indo-Pak War, over Bangladesh, was even appreciated by the enemy. During the 1965 and 1971 Indo-Pak Wars in the Western Sector, its fire power was instrumental in breaking the Pakistani Armoured and Infantry. It was also used in our strategic response against the Chinese at Nathu-la, in Sikkim, in September 1967 with devastating results. Fighting obsolescence with great determination, the gun continued to serve with Medium Regiments in the High Himalayas, up to the 1990s, till it finally retired in 1997 from 25 Infantry Division Sector of Jammu and Kashmir. Pakistan Artillery continued to use it in the Siachen glacier, and also during the 1999 war in the Kargil sector. Technical details of the gun :

(a)	Range	16550 metres
(b)	Weight of shell	36.3 kilograms
(c)	Lethality	46 metres
(d)	Weight of gun	12,766 kilograms
(e)	Intense rate of fire	2 rounds per minute

5.5 Inch Gun

Kraz 214B

A jat sikh, Medium Gunner, Naib Subedar Baldev Singh, Modelling As a Quintenssential Medium Gunner (Height 6 Feet and 6 Inches, plus one centimetre), With The 5.5 inch Gun, At The Heritage Park, School of Artillery, Devlali.

Appendix C

(Refer to Note 5, Chapter 1)

Some Selected Ranks of 27 (Poonch) Medium Battery and others

1. **Major CP Khopkar:** He was called 'Charu' by all. A handsome and suave officer, from Bombay who had applied for resignation from the army. He had seen action with the regiment, during 1965, and was respected by the troops. He left the army on release during August 1971, and has since settled in Australia.

2. **Major MC Ramanand:** A young officer (YO) of the Regiment, like Charu Khopkar. Took command of 27(Poonch) Medium Battery, on August 28, 1971, from Charu Khopkar. Had been Gun Position Officer (GPO), during the 1965 War. A cool brave battery Commander, who sat in the open, on the Squadron Commander's (Major Inderjit Singh) tank, of 1 (Independent) Armoured Squadron from November to December, 1971, as a Medium battery Commander, .in support of armour. True to his spirit, his son, Second Lieutenant Dhiraj Ramanand, joined the Regiment, after passing out from the 100th Indian Military Academy Course, in June 1997.

3. **Captain A R Pedgaonkar:** An energetic go-getter, full of fight. He was a good task master, and was very daring, under enemy fire (may be small arms or artillery). Died

of airburst splinters during operations in Belonia, in November 1971, as Observation Post Officer, with 14th Battalion the Kumaon Regiment.

4. **Captain RS Sandhu:** Joined the battery on posting, from Artillery Centre, Nasik Road, as battery Second-in Command on November 24, 1971. A short and softspoken person, he moved as Observation Post Officer (link sign 45) with 1st Battalion, 11 Gorkha Rifles (1/11 GR) till fall of Chandpur, and later as Observer with 8 BIHAR and 9 KUMAON.

5. **Captain RC Wolfe:** A Young Officer (YO) of the regiment. A good footballer and a guitarist. Was one of the first observers from the unit to operate with 10 BIHAR, during October 1971 action by *Mukti Bahini,* at Kasba / Saldanadi, where the Regiment was part of 57 Mountain Division. During November to December 1971, he was permanently attached with the Infantry (3 DOGRA of 83 Mountain Brigade). After fall of Laksham, though out of the range of medium guns, he had to continue to give observation and liaison and proceeded towards the thrust down South, by 83 Mountain Brigade for capture of Feni / Chittagong, till he rejoined the battery by hitch-hiking on December 14,1971, after being called back from Feni.

6. **Subedar (Driver Special Vehicle) Fakir Singh:** He was the Senior Junior Commissioned Officer (JCO) of the battery. Had seen service in North West Frontier Province, before partition, and was having more than 20 years of service. He was a self-taught Gun Position Officer (GPO), and performed the job of GPO of D troop, in November - December 1971, admirably. Was at his element when it came to recovery of bogged down vehicles and guns, in the soft patches.

7. **Naib Subedar (Operator) Hardip Singh:** A Regimental basketball player of ferocious temperament. He could outplay or outride the opponent with his elbow, without the referee noticing it, and was nicknamed *Konha*

(elbow). Had been an Instructor in the Signal Wing, at Military College of Telecommunication Engineering, at Mhow, and was convinced as an Instructor that, in civil, current flows from negative to positive, and vice versa in 'fauj' (army). Was a self-taught Gun Position Officer (GPO) and performed the duties of GPO of C Troop.

8. **The Gun Numbers One:** The gun numbers one or detachment commanders were :

(a) No. 1 Gun (C1)	–	Havaldar Jit Singh, was called 'Amli' for his occasional love of poppy seeds, with incessant tea drinking.
(b) No. 2 Gun (C2)	–	Havaldar Mohinder Singh (90). The most outstanding, Non Commissioned Officer.
(c) No.3 Gun (C3)	–	Havaldar Kehar Singh, very religious. His gun had the maximum direct hits on enemy.
(d) No. 4 Gun (D1)	–	Havaldar Mohinder Singh (70). Smart and effective.
(e) No. 5 Gun (D2)	–	Havaldar Kabal Singh, a born junior leader under fire.
(f) No. 6 Gun (D3)	–	Havaldar Joginder Singh (31), a Services Hockey Player.
(g) Ammunition Havaldar	–	Havaldar Jagdish Singh, 'Ammunition'- the real weapon of the gunners was always under his efforts.

9. **Battery Havaldar Major (BHM) Pargat Singh:** The senior most Non Commissioned Officer, had a good control on the men.

10. **Driver Operator Gurcharan Singh:** Was the battery Commander's operator and travelled piggy back on the

PT-76 Tank of Squadron Commander of 1 (Independent) Armoured Squadron. Was Mentioned in Despatches for keeping the radio through, under adverse conditions while operating with the tanks.

11. **Vehicle Mechanic Raghubir:** He was permanently attached from the Light Repair Workshop of the Electrical Mechanical Engineers (EME). Was a wizard in repairing broken down Krazes and winches.

12. **Battery Quartermaster Havaldar Malkit Singh:** A basketballer of repute. Was smart and sophisticated and always neatly dressed, most probably due to his 'quartermaster' background. Could speak fluent English on the radio.

13. **Lance Naik (Cook) Kheela Singh:** Not to be mixed up with the *Jat* Sikh Singh. Kheela Singh was *Jat* from Haryana. Come what may, he always produced hot meals in the Wagon Lines. The noise of his oil cooker was sometimes mistaken with that of a jet aircraft! During lulls in cooking, he would visit the guns, and help in firing the gun, as a hobby.

14. **Lance Naik (Operator) Ranjit Singh:** The key Radio Operator in the Command Post - never missed to receive or transmit any orders and information on the radio set. Was code named 'Bau' - a term still incomprehensible.

15. **Technical Assistant Havaldar Nachattar Singh:** He was code named 'Marhia' by the gunners due to his thin and wiry built. Day or night, he could record and align the guns in the required azimuth or bearing in excellent time.

16. **Lance Naik Major Singh:** The tough ammunition gunner of C2 gun. Could lift as many rounds on his back, as ordered.

17. **Naik Darshan Singh:** Was the second-in-Command of C2 gun. An exceptionally good layer of the gun and a patient instructor.

Other Personalities

1. **Major Harbhajan Singh:** He was the second-in-command of 57 Mountain Regiment. During the Belonia operations, 27 (Poonch) Medium battery had operated as the fourth or Sierra battery of 57 Mountain Regiment. Major Harbhajan Singh was responsible for deployment at the gun-end, however, he had one quality and that was his offensive spirit. He was so much fired with the zeal to close-up with the enemy that, as a matter of habit, he used to visit the Observation Posts, and troops in forward localities, in close proximity to the enemy and engage them with fire. He was injured twice due to his relish of enemy fire - once with a burst of light machine gun, and another time, with a splinter from a mine. He later commanded 24 Medium Regiment (SP) in the 1980s. He retired as a Brigadier and died in an unfortunate road accident. He was instrumental in reviving games and sports in the unit and insisted that all battery teams must be under 25 years of age, to allow young blood to flower.
2. **Major General RD Hira:** This General Officer, commanding 23 Mountain Division often visited the gun position in November. He always gave a pat to the medium gunners. He was well versed in 'fire discipline' or the language of fire control of the gunners. To each command of 'stand fast', given by the Gun Position Officer - he said 'Go on'. Was a hero amongst the troops.
3. **Brigadier Satnam Singh Opal:** He was the Commander of Artillery 23 Mountain Artillery Brigade. He had been the Commanding Officer of 24 Medium Regiment during the 1965 war and knew the men and the gun like the back of his palm. He employed the regiment ideally, to suit the peculiar nature of the operations.

'Mukti Bahini'

The quintessential, 'peace loving and non martial' image which we may have had, of the *lungi* clad and bare-footed

East-Bengali, was dispelled the moment we saw them in action, against the Pakistani Army. The *Mukti Bahini* was a motley collection of ex-soldiers, ex-policemen, students and others. Being part of the Scythian and established martial race of Sikh troops, it was a pleasant surprise to see these brave people. We soon realised that, any human, who is subjected to unjust treatment and atrocities, can metamorphose into a ferocious *guerrilla fighter.*

The *Mukti Bahini* was of great assistance in navigation and intelligence gathering. Their domination was in the countryside, and during the final stages of the war, they had restricted the free and unhindered movement of Pakistani troops, mobile reserves and patrols - much to the advantage of the Indian Army.

Obituary

At the conclusion of the 1971 war, the gunners who had laid down their lives, are listed. In 1997, a book *Amar Jawan* was released, which has details of all battle casualties and accidents, but not deaths due to sickness. The roll of honour includes :

Date of Death/Casualty	Service Number	Name	Cause of Casualty
Oct. 23, 1971	1195506	Gunner Narang Singh of 243 Medium battery	Pakistan Artillery
Oct. 25, 1971	1192397	Gunner Gurbhej Singh	Drowned while on a patrol
Nov. 17, 1971	IC-22207	Captain AR Pedgaonkar	Pakistan Artillery
Dec. 24, 1971	1187464	Driver Sukhdev Singh	Vehicle accident
Not exactly known	1226494	Vehicle Fitter Artillery Gurmukh Singh	Water borne Disease/ Recorded Sickness

Source: Adapted from Nayyar, KK, Vice Admiral (Retired), *Amar Jawan: " A Book of Remembrance,* Indian Book House Publishers, New Delhi, 1997, p.188).

Appendix D

(Refer to Notes in Table 1)

Details of Artillery Equipment—Indian

Sl. No.	Equipment (Crew or Gun Detach-ments)	Prime Mover or Field Artillery Tractor or GunTowing Vehicle	Weight in kilo-grams	Maximum Range/ Planning Range (Meters)	Highest Rate of Fire	Shell Weight
1.	5.5 inch Gun (09)	Kraz 214B	12768	16550 13250	2 rounds per minute	80pounds (36.3 Kgs)
2.	75/24 Pack Howitzer (06)	1 Ton or Mules Artillery	983	11104 8900	5 rounds per minute	6.052 Kgs
3.	76 mm M48B1 (Yugoslav Mountain Gun) (06)	—	690	8600 6900	"	6.2 Kgs.
4.	120 mm Brandt Mortar (06)	—	421	6515 5200	10 Bombs per minute	13.2 Kgs

Notes

1. Pakistan Artillery was equipped with 105 mm (Italian) Howitzer, having a maximum range of 11,300 metres and shell weight of 15 kilograms.
2. The mountain guns were often moved in various modes of draught, including, being pulled and pushed manually. Movement for these guns was never a problem.
3. The 120 mm Brandt Mortars, also called 'heavy mortars' were even easier to move. At some places, they were even carried on PT 76 tanks of 1 (Independent) Armoured Squadron.

Appendix E

(Refer to Chapter IV, Page 53)

Gunnery Problems Encountered

During the Belonia operations, as live firing was carried out, a number of interesting Gunnery *Ghundis* (or complex questions which always have answers) came up. Some gunnery problems encountered, were :

(a) The maximum range of charge super of 5.5 inch Gun was 18100 yards and the maximum range of the rage arm of artillery board was, 16,000 yards. The use of Convertor Field Artillery, at ranges beyond 16,000 yards, was found to be very useful, in following target grid Corrections. The Junior Commissioned Officers, who performed as Gun Position Officers, were very proficient in their use.

(b) Generally in certain setpiece attacks, registration of objectives is done by firing before the attack. Also, once guns are re-recorded from day to night, it is insisted that parallelism of guns must be checked. In one such incidence, targets were registered, just before dark. After registration, the guns had to record night centre of arc. It was discovered that on checking parallelism, nearly all guns were having some deviations. The tricky question was, whether to re-record the guns by passing a fresh bearing, or not to disturb the setting on the sights. According to the theoretical textbook teachings, the former is advocated, but in accordance with practical situation, one realised that, as the guns had already reached the target, with the Quadrant Elevation (QE) and bearing or azimuth, and changes now would mean trouble. The second option was adopted, and the fire was accurate. Of course, on capture of objective, the guns were quickly re-recorded.

(c) Each round must be predicted to land as close as possible to the target. In one such case, a last round to get the guns empty, before moving to the next position, was fired using Rough and Ready meteorological methods, on a suspected enemy locality, near Feni. Later we learnt that, a single round had caused heavy casualties to the Baluch battalion.

(d) At times, while recording the guns with a director, all the sights are not visible from the director, because of lie of grounds and other reasons. During such eventualities, a gun can be recorded from its neighbouring gun, using the dial sight. This procedure was called 'Dial Sight' method.

(e) There were occasions when the Indian Maps of 1 inch to 1 mile (scale 1:63,360), where one map square was 1000 yards, got mixed up with captured Pakistani Metric Maps of 1:50,000 (1 Square = 1000 m). It became difficult to correlate the two, and the same point on ground gave different coordinates or grid reference. Mix up of maps was avoided, although it was found that, the 1:50,000 metric maps had more details and were more accurate.

(f) Avoid siting guns under trees, as the tree, if hit by a ground burst shell of enemy, makes the shell burst in the air, and causes more casualties to a gun detachment in the open.

(g) In mobile operations guns commence firing soon on deployment. Digging and preparing a second gun pit, next to the gun in action, is not practical, instead gunners find it convenient to dig down by ingenuity and improvisation the gun from its existing position by skilful use of digging tools and jacks. Dug down guns always give protection against ground bursts. In war everybody digs.

(h) As the medium guns have longer range than the field or mountain guns, generally in peace time discussions, the guns are deployed in depth, generally as a rule, behind the mountain or field guns. However, in actual operations and war, the medium guns are deployed forward, as far as possible, and generally, ahead of even the mountain or field guns, to reach at depth or interdiction targets.

(j) Operational or Deployment orders are generally given in bits and pieces. The full formats, as taught during peace, is seldom possible due to fluid nature of battle. Generally, only the centre of arc was stated, and the gun area was given in a general area - due to bad going, at times where one got stuck, it became the gun area.

(k) Although, tannoy is a device to pass fire orders to the guns by the Gun Position Officer, it was realised that, during shelling and fire plans, it was prudent for the Gun Position Officer or Troop Leaders to come out of dug in shelter and use a megaphone and shout the orders. It may sound foolhardy, but sight of a leader in the open, giving orders, is a great morale booster to the gun-crew. Hoarse throats are occupational hazards.

(l) Often in discussions, it was said that, the small calibre mountain gun was a 'Pea Shooter' etc. Nevertheless, at the receiving end it was a totally different story. The bursting of even a shell of a mountain gun near one, causes enough moral and physiological damage, and achieves the aim of neutralisation.

Appendix F

(Refer to Chapter 5, Footnote, p.85)

Sportsmanship and War

24 Medium Regiment had produced three national level sportsmen, in the mid-1960s, and they were, Naib Subedar Jit Singh, in High Jump; battery Havaldar Major Gurnam Singh, in Hop, Step and Jump; and Naib Subedar Balbir Singh, in Hammer Throw. As a result of this unique and rare contribution to the army, the Directorate General of Artillery, at Army Headquarters, had presented a special trophy to the regiment. The Regiment had an outstanding record in all fields of sports, and nearly every discipline of athletics and other games had a services-level representative from the regiment. It had also been established beyond doubt that, a unit which excelled in sports, also did well in the war. One legend, regarding battery Havaldar Major Gurnam Singh was that, he went to the extent of crossing the border, and attempted to enroll in the Pakistan Army - only to set a new national Pakistan record in Triple Jump.

All these three athletes were serving in the regiment, and soon after cease-fire, they came to know that, certain Prisoners of War of Pakistan Army, who were also sportsmen, and whom they had met earlier in various Dual Meets (Indo-Pak sports fixtures), had been interned in camps near Kakraban which probably included Subedar Abdul Khaliq, the Pakistani champion of 100 and 200 Metres Dash. There was an immediate request from the three sportsmen to meet them, and enquire about their well-being:

Brigadier Atif, during the surrender had shown the true spirit of sportsmanship. Being an Olympic player of repute, he had the magnanimity to give 24 Medium Regiment, a compliment called "good shooting".

To complete the compliments, it was indeed the gunners of 53 Field Regiment of Pakistan Artillery, which in spite of heavy odds, had created many an uncomfortable moments for the battery at Belonia, and then at Buschi, near Laksham.

Later in 2001, the Hamoodur Rehman Report was available on the internet. I was extremely disappointed to learn that, the Commanding Officer of 53 Field Regiment, had charges of Human Rights Atrocities against him, during the so-called "Suppression of the Mutiny".

---

* This name, I recall from my hazy memory. I could not contact our sportsmen to cross-check and confirm this information. In 1997, Captain SS Gill, the Officer Commanding Boys Sports Company of Artillery Centre, Hyderabad, of mid 1960s enrolment, confirmed that, it must have been him. Any mistake is unintentional. In 2002, in NOIDA, Brigadier N Bahri (Retd.I. from the GUARDS, who had been a missile company commander, as a Major in 26 Infantry Divisional Sector, confirmed that, one Abdul Khaliq had been taken prisoner in the western sector, in the area of operations of 26 Infantry Division.

Annotated Bibliography

General

I have attempted to keep these memoirs of a subaltern as simple and spontaneous as possible. With the scholarly hindsight, it became impossible not to refer to books written 10, 20 or even 30 years after the event. To keep the essence of this sort of a 'subaltern study' alive, most of the secondary sources in the chapters and appendices, have been given as endnotes. The rule followed is that, any operation, incidence or event, during the war, which is mentioned in this book and which has also been referred to in another book, has been indicated in the endnotes. Inconsistencies in dates and even reporting on events are expected.

As larger number of books and information became available after the initial draft, I thought it would be better to insert an epilogue or a bibliographical essay. Bibliographical Essay, I realised, would be easier to compile. There was a strong inclination to rewrite the book, but then, it would not have been what I wanted it to be. I plan to write a book on the strategic pattern, which may now emerge on our military experience, since independence.

Bibliography

A number of books have since been written, on the political and other backgrounds of the 1971 War, which ultimately led to the Indo-Pak War, and the creation of Bangladesh, in December 1971. Readers can refer to the under-mentioned books, giving the various versions on the 1971 War in Bangladesh. This is not an exhaustive list, but only what I could compile:

Official Indian History

The only official military histories, as in the year 2006, which are available on our wars with other countries, are the operations in Jammu and Kashmir 1947-1948, and against the Portuguese, in the liberation of Goa in 1961. It was learnt that in the early 1990s, selected senior appointments in the Service Headquarters were provided with the official copy of the 1971 war. It was not made public. In the year 2000, the *Times of India* group of newspapers, had placed on the internet, the official histories of the 1965 and 1971 Indo-Pakistan Wars, through probably investigative journalism (www.timesofindia.com). From newspaper reports it emerged that the history is a 874 page typescript, in two parts, which was ready in 1992. The General Editor, SN Prasad, in an interview disclosed that in 1983, he was commissioned to write the 1971 war history, and then, he also completed the 1962 Sino-Indian War, and the 1965 Indo–Pakistan War (See Manoj Joshi, 'War and History', *Times of India,* December 2, 2000).

Relevant extracts from this source, covering the Battle of Belonia, is at Annexure to this Appendix. This gives a wholesome picture to these preliminary operations.

In the year 2004, it was decided that, the Historical Division of Ministry of Defence would release the Histories of the 1962, 1965 and the 1971 Wars. But prior to their release, they were required to be updated and further edited. The Centre of Armed Forces Historical Research (CAFHR) which was established in the year 2001, at the. United Service Institution of India, New Delhi, has begun updating the histories of the 1962, 1965 and 1971 wars. All are now forthcoming. It is learnt that, these would not be the 'Official Histories'.

I can offer one comment, not as a subaltern, but as a student of strategy, on the war in Bangladesh. Although Dacca was not specified in orders, it became the objective, when opportunity arose. Initially, it was not given out clearly, as the final objective. This is one of the reasons why, multiple objectives are considered in a breakout. This opportunistic action, indicated that, mobility of the mind is more important. An armed force, which quickly adjusts to meet and seize fleeting situations, comes out the best. This is what is called, *Auftgastaktik,* or directive control.

A Note on Maps

The standard of maps in most of the books published in India, do not give a proper idea of space and the terrain. In general, maps in Indian publications, are not accurate and self explanatory. It is hoped that, officials concerned will publish better maps, even if they are branded as 'not to scale'.

Indian Authors

1. Bhaumik, Subin, *Insurgents Cross Fire: North-East India,* New Delhi, Lancers Publishers, 1996. The author gives an account of the decision-making and the sequence of events, in support of the *Mukti Bahini.* He gives, June 19,1971, as the first day, when trans-border guerilla raid on Lathitilla was given artillery support by the Indian Army. According to the author, by around September 1971, there were 60 training camps, and about 20,000 personnel were being trained per month (pp.33-35).

2. Chaudhury, Rahul Roy, *Sea Power and Indian Security,* London, Brassey's, 1995. Indian assistance and maritime training to the *Mukti Bahini,* including the famous landward side raid on Chittagong, Chalna, Mangla and Khulna, on August 15, 1971, have been mentioned.

3. Dixit, JN, *Liberation and Beyond,* New Delhi, Konark Publishers, 1999. The author alludes to the joint-command and control between the Indian military headquarters, and the Bangladesh Government in exile. According to the author, the Indian military involvement commenced from October 1971 (p.88).

4. Chopra, Pran, *India's Second Liberation,* Vikas Publishing House Private Limited, 1973.

5. Dinesh, AM, *India Wins the War;* Oriental Publishers, Pataudi House, Daryaganj, Delhi. 1972.

6. Ganguly, Rajat, *Kin State Intervention in Ethnic Conflict* New Delhi, Sage Publishers, 1998. The author has covered India's policy and its support to the 'Bengali Freedom Movement', both covert and overt.

7. Ganguly, Sumit.

   (a) *The Origins of War in South Asia : Indo-Pakistan Conflicts Since* 1947. Westview Special Studies on South and Southeast Asia, 1986.

   (b) *Conflict Unending: Indo-Pakistan Tension Since* 1947, New Delhi, Oxford University Press. The author mentions that, by late October 1971, India started to exert steady military pressure on Pakistan. On November 22, Indian Forces, along the border areas of East-Pakistan, had started to provide Artillery Fire to project *Mukti Bahini* forces.

8. Garg, SK, Captain, *Spotlight: Freedom Fighters of Bangladesh,* New Delhi, Allied Publishers Private Limited, 1984. Probably one of the few books written about the *Mukti Bahini;* by an Indian author.

9. Jacob, JFR, Lieutenant General, *Surrender at Dacca: Birth of a Nation,* Manohar Publishers, New Delhi, 1997. Units and Formations of 23 and 57 Mountain Divisions, appearing at Tables 1 and 2, have been cross-checked from this book. This is one of the few books, written by a senior Lieutenant General, who was the Chief of Staff of Headquarters Eastern Command, during the war. This is a good "top down" perspective, unlike the "bottom up" view of this book.

10. Kadian, Rajesh, *India and its Army,* Vision Books, 1990, (pp. 58-64).

11. Kathpalia, PN, Lieutenant General, *Mission with a Difference: The Exploits of* 71 *Mountain Brigade.* Lancer International, New Delhi. The author was a Brigade Commander in the Northern Sector.

12. Lal, PC, Air Chief Marshal, *My Years with the IAF,* Ela Lal (Edited), Lancers International, New Delhi, 1986. The author was the Chief of the Air Staff during the war. A classic.

13. Mankekar, DR, *Pakistan Cut to Size,* Indian Book Company, 19/20 Windsor Mansion, Janpath Lane, New Delhi, 1972.

14. Mohd Ayub and K Subrahmanyam, *The Liberation War;* S Chand and Company (Private) Limited, Ram Nagar, New Delhi, 1972.

15. Nanda, AK, Admiral, *The Man Who Bombed Karachi;* New Delhi, 2004. The author was the Chief of the Naval Staff and provides a fascinating account on the planning and execution of the naval operations, and also the decision-making at the highest level.

16. Nanda, KK, Lieutenant General (Retd.). *Conquering Kashmir; A Pakistani Obsession,* Lancer Books, 1994.

17. Nath, Rajendra, Major General, *Military Leadership India, Vedic Period to Indo-Pak Wars,* Lancers Books, 1990. The author has devoted an entire section to 4 Corps-operations (pp.511-530). This is one of the few accounts of the corps. The author has praised the Generalship of the Corps Commander, Lieutenant General Sagat Singh. His interview with senior Pakistani officers, prisoners of war, on the role of *Mukti Bahini* and its effect on operations, has been termed as minimal. This may be a variance with what has been recorded in these memoirs.

18. Nayar, Kuldip. *Distant Neighbours, A Tale of the Subcontinent,* Vikas Publishing House (Private) Limited, 1972.

19. Nayyar, KK, Vice Admiral (Retd.), *Amar Jawan: A Book of Rememberance,* New Delhi, India Book House Publishers, 1997. This book records all the battle casualties (fatal), since independence.

20. Palit, DK, Major General.

(a) *The Lightning Campaign,* Thomson Press (India) Limited, New Delhi, 1972. The author was the Director, Military Operations, at Army Headquarters, during 1962 Sino-Indian War. This is the prescribed textbook for promotion examinations for junior army officers.

(b) Later, in 1991, the author wrote *The War in the High Himalayas,* New Delhi, Lancers Publishers, 1991. In this book, the author removed the sheen from the blitzkrieg and lightning campaign thesis, which was mentioned by him in the former book. He criticised the delay to launch operations in the winter. Early spring or summer, according to the author, should have been a better option. The author also compares the plan of the 1971 war, in the east, to the insipid moves of the stalemated 1965 Indo-Pakistan War on the western front. The author's argument goes against the Army Chief's advise to await logistics preparation, and the onset of winter, in order to deny the Chinese any approach during winter. Somehow, a quick response sort of an Army, has often been desired. Ever since, and after the Indian mobilisation in December 2001, during 'Operation Parakram' against Pakistan, there has been a debate on a rapid standby sort of an organisation for a swift blow. However, keeping the practical terrain and operation configuration, it would take a long time to keep an army fully equipped and psyched for a tripwire sort of a response.

21. Rao, Krishna, General, *Prepare or Perish,* Lancer Publishers, 1991. The author was General Officer Commanding, 8 Mountain Division, which was the Northern pincer of IV Corps.

22. Rushdie, Salman, *Midnight's Children,* Bard Books, Avon Books, 1982. Though a work of fiction, it has interesting

anecdotes and situations, tracing the camaraderie between senior Indian and Pakistani Generals, who were part of the great British Indian Army, before the partition. See Book Three.

23. Saigal, J R, Lieutenant Colonel

    (a) *New Light On India, China & India Pakistan Wars: The Invisible Factor,* Defence Seminar Publications, NOIDA, 1998. The author feels that, Lt. Gen. Sagat Singh was not given the due importance, after the war, though IV Corps was instrumental in the campaign, and the final fall of Dacca. According to the author, Sagat Singh had performed well during the Goa operations and the Indian response with fire fights in Sikkim in 1967 against the Chinese.

    (b) *Pakistan Splits: The Birth of Bangladesh;* New Delhi, Manas Publications, 2000. The author has compared the Generalship of Lieutenant General Sagat Singh, the General Officer Commanding of IV Corps, to that of the legendary German Field Marshall Erwin Romell, by calling him a "Mini Romell" of the Indian Army. See p.185. Operations of IV Corps undoubtedly are a good case–study of operational art in the Indian context.

24. Sandhu, Gurcharan Singh, Major General (Retd.), *The Indian Armour: History of the Indian Armoured Corps* (1941-1971). Vision Books Private Limited, 1987. Chapter 22, (pp.468-480).

25. Singh, Depinder, Lieutenant General, PVSM, VSM, *Field Marshal Sam Manekshaw: Soldiering with Dignity;* Natraj Publishers, 2002, Dehradun. The author was the Military Assistant to the Army Chief. This biography of the Chief of the Army Staff, provided insights into the decision-making and the leadership style. The famous incidence of the Chief, insisting on the postponement of the campaign to winter, to the then Prime Minister is recorded here. Manekshaw in private, had asked the Prime Minister, whether he should claim insanity and

resign. Indira Gandhi, the then Prime Minister, had rejected the offer, telling him that, he was absolutely right. (p.129).

26. Singh, Jagdev, Brigadier, *Dismemberment of Pakistan: 1971 Indo-Pak War,* Lancer International, 1988. The author was the Chief Engineer at Headquarters IV Corps.

27. Singh, Lachman, Major General, *Victory in Bangladesh,* Natraj Publisher, 1981, and *Indian Sword Strikes in East-Pakistan,* Vikas Publishing House Private Limited, 1979. The former book covers all the sectors or fronts. The latter, is exclusively the battle accounts of 20 Mountain Division, from the perception of a General Officer Commanding, which the author was. These are amongst the prescribed books for the Army promotion examinations.

28. Singh, Sarbans, Major (Retd.), Psc, *Battle Honours of the Indian Army,* New Delhi, Vision Books, 1993. 2 Rajput was given the Battle Honour, "Belonia".

29. Singh, Sukhwant, Major General, *The Liberation of Bangladesh,* Vikas Publishing House Private Limited, 1981. The author was a Deputy, in the rank of a Brigadier, in the Military Operations Directorate, at Army Headquarters, during the war. His book was published posthumously, and contains a number of insights and opinions.

30. Singh, VK, Major General (Retd.), *Leadership in the Indian Army: Biographies of Twelve Solidiers,* Sage Publishers, 2005. The book has an entire chapter devoted to Lt Gen Sagat Singh the General Officer Commanding IV Corps and the outstanding performance of the troops under his command. See Chapter 9. pp. 293-325.

31. Sondhi, SS, Brigadier (Retd.), *Operation Wind Fall: Emergence of Bangladesh.* Allied Publishers Private Limited, 1980, and *Top Brass: A Critical Appraisal of the Indian Military Leadership,* Trishul Publication,

NOIDA (India), 1993. The author was Commander of 301 Mountain Brigade of 23 Mountain Division, under IV Corps. A detailed account of the operations of the Brigade, including his views and comments, are covered in *Operation Windfall.* From IV Corps zone, he may be the only Brigade Commander, who has written a book. None of the GOCs in IV Corps Zone have penned anything substantial.

32. Subrahmanyam, K, *Bangladesh and India's Security;* Compiled and Published by Major General DK Palit, Palit and Dutt Publishers, Dehradun, 1972. A series of newspaper articles and seminar papers of K Subrahmanyam, as Director of the Institute for Defence Studies and Analyses (IDSA), before the war, suggesting that, it would be more economical to fight a war to solve the problem of Bangladesh, than to feed millions of refugees, indefinitely. A must read for students, who want to study the evolution of strategic thought in India. Another aspect, which the author brings out is the role of the United Nations. He alluded to the bitter lesson that India learnt, when it took the dispute over Jammu and Kashmir to the UN, over the war with Pakistan, in 1947-1948. Thereafter, according to the author, India did not take the issue of Goa (1961), the Chinese attack in 1962, Pakistan's attack in Kutch in April 1965, and their attack in Kashmir in August 1965 to the international community for a solution. India tried to tackle all these security issues on bilateral basis, with her own efforts. In a piece titled, 'Pakistani Options', in June 1971, he wrote, "that the Pakistani military leadership would prefer to fight it out, rather than enter into a political settlement. One hounorable way out for them," he elaborated, "is a war with India. They can at the end of it, still preserve their image, and tell the West Pakistani people that Bangladesh was detached from Pakistan, not as a result of any failure on their part, but because of the superior military might of India."

33. Tewari, KK, Major General (Retd.), *A Soldier's Voyage of Self Discovery.* Aoroville, Pondicherry, All India Press, 1995. The author was the Chief Signals Officer at the Eastern Command Headquarters, and provides fascinating political, military, technical and spiritual insights.

34. Verma, Kalyan, Major General (Retd.), *Rivers of Silence,* New Delhi, Lancers Publishers, 1997. The author was commanding 18 RAJPUT, under 57 Mountain Division.

35. Verma, HN, and Verma, Amit, *Decisive Battles of India,* Volume II, California GIP Books, 1998. According to the authors, Indian assistance to the *Mukti Bahini,* began from April 1971 and they were given training from July to October.

Published Regimental Histories

Unlike official history of the Ministry of Defence, Government of India, which is still not available, the Indian Navy and Regiments and Corps of the Indian Army, have complied their histories. The following is a list of known books to the author of units and formations, that took part in the operations from the IV Corps Front.

1. Das, Chand, Major General, *The Rajputana Rifles: Brief History,* Reliance Publishing House, New Delhi, 1995.

2. Gautam Sharma, Lieutenant Colonel, *The History of the Jat Regiment* (1947-1972), Volume III. Allied Publishers Private Limited, New Delhi, 1979.

3. Hiranandani, GM, Vice Admiral, *Transition to Triumph: History of the Indian Navy, 1965-75,* Naval Headquarters, New Delhi, Lancers Publishers, 1999. The history gives details on the naval raids by the *Mukti Bahini* naval guerillas. The sequence of events and political and military decision-making has been covered in details. The political decision to prepare for military intervention according to this book, in case a satisfactory political solution had not been found, was taken as early as April, 1971.

4. *History of Army Service Corps, Volume* 5 (1947-1976). Directorate of Supplies and Transport, Army Headquarters, Sterling Publishers, 1977.

5. *History of the Electrical and Mechanical Engineers.* Directorate of EME, 1981. This account has the best maps.

6. Khanna, RB, Colonel:

   (a) *The Sapper's War,* Engineer-in-Chief Directorate, 1995.

   (b) *God's Own: The Bengal Sappers,* Baroj Khanna, Jaipur, 2003. Two Bengal Sappers units took part in the operations in IV Corps zone. 62 Engineer Regiment, in support of 23 Mountain Division, and 234 Engineer Regiment, in support of 57 Mountain Division. The book records that Field Companies of 62 Engineer Regiment were grouped with assaulting brigades in addition to their own affiliated Field Companies, from 3 Engineer Regiment. The book reconstructs the episode at Buschi of December 6, and mentions that due to a communication bottleneck-cum-traffic jam of advancing vehicles, it was an easy artillery target. Accordingly, it was punished by Pakistani observation post, and in the shelling, 35 vehicles were destroyed. In the melee, GOC 23 Mountain Division had a narrow escape, when exploding shells from burning vehicles landed on his jeep. The engineers, as the book records, undertook to making a bypass through forests in bad going and exploding shells (pp.265-267).

7. Mehra, KC. *A History of the Ordnance Corps,* Directorate of Ordnance, Army Headquarters, Wheeler Publications, 1980.

8. Mukherjee, Anjan, Colonel, *God of War: History of the Regiment of Artillery* 1966-1999, Directorate General of Artillery, in association with Lancers Publishers and Distributors, 2003. Surprisingly, in this book, no mention

of the Open Action at Hajiganj by 27 (Poonch) Medium battery, on December 8, has been done, as given in Chapter V and Sketch 2. An article by me, in the *Royal Artillery Journal* of UK, in its Autumn 2002 issue, also features this famous action. The action by some compilation oversight, or mystery, has been attributed to 197 Mountain Regiment (p.80). Probably, the incidence was not properly recorded in the after action report, filed by the regimental Headquarters of 24 Medium Regiment, which was far back, and also involved in other duties like that of counter-bombardment command post. Being both a general support medium battery and in direct support to the independent armoured squadron, many actions of the medium gunners could have been taken for granted, or not recorded, as with our long range, we could fire for more than one mountain brigade. Each action of a mountain brigade was seen from the perspective of the direct support mountain regiment. In case of the open action, the brigade advancing was 301 Mountain Brigade, which had 197 mountain regiment, as the direct support unit. This procedure, for recording battle actions, could be the reason for this sort of a fake encounter, now recorded by historians, as that carried out by a mountain regiment.

9. Palsokar, RD, Colonel, *The Bihar Warriors : Historical Records of Bihar Regiment* 1986. See, History of 8 BIHAR, Chapter 23.

10. Palsokar, RD, Colonel, *The Dogra Regiment: A Saga of Gallantry and Valour,* Published under arrangements with Commandant, Dogra Regimental Centre, Faizabad, 1982. For an account of the attack on Parshuram, in November 1971, by 3 DOGRA, by then a commanding officer, see Major General AS Chopra, *Reminiscences of a Battalion Commander, Sainik Samachar,* Volume 44, No.7, April 1-15, 1997. The author narrates the incidence, when a direct hit of an artillery round, from a Medium Gun, on the Mike Party (Line Laying Party)

of 57 Mountain Regiment, as also on troops of 3 Dogra, resulted in seven killed. The Pakistan Artillery did not have any medium guns. The round was probably from the 105 mm field guns of 53 Field Regiment of Pakistan Artillery. 2/Lt Rajiv Sarin (now a Brigadier) and my course-mate was also in 3 Dogra, though I met him nearly 25 years after the war.

11. Praval, KC, *Valour Triumphs: A History of the Kumaon Regiment,* Thomson Press (India) Limited, 1976. My dear friend and course-mate 2/Lt DK Das of 12 Kumaon, was killed during reorganisation, due to Pakistan artillery shelling, in operations of 57 Mountain Division.

12. Prasad, Shankar, Lt Gen(Retd), *The Gallant Dogras: An Illustrated History of the Dogra Regiment.* Dogra Regimental Centre, published in India by Lancer Publishers 2005. This coffe table book features the actions of 3 Dogra, see pp. 144-146.

13. Proud-foot, CL, Lieutenant Colonel (Retd.), Editor, *We Lead 7th Light Cavalry* 1784-1990. Lancer International, 1991, Chapter 14, pp. 201-216.

14. Sethna, AM, Lieutenant General and Katju Valmiki, Lieutenant Colonel, *Traditions of a Regiment,* Lancer Publishers, 1983. The book covers the history of Rajputana Rifles.

15. Sharma, Gautam, Lieutenant Colonel, *Path of Glory: Exploits of* 11 *Gorkha Rifles,* Allied Publishers Private Limited, 1979, 2/Lt Bhanwar Singh, my course-mate was in the 1/11 GR Battalion.

16. Sharma, Gautam, Lieutenant Colonel, *The History of the Jat Regiment (1947-1972), Volume III,* Allied Publishers 1979.

17. Subramanyam, VA, Colonel, *The Signals: A History of the Corps of Signals.* Directorate General of Signals, Army Headquarters, Macmillan India Limited, New Delhi, 1986. The false alarm, referred to by me, in Chapter

III, at the Gazaria observation post (OP), with 10 Bihar in October 1971, of a surprise Pakistani attack finds a mention in this history (p.175). Also, the futility of an elaborate electronic deception plan at the highest level has been mentioned. The plan was called off due to lack of resources. The history records that the staff and commanders realised that strategic and tactical deception is a specialsed job and such operations need to be credible (p.177). The deception by firing a single gun at Belonia in November 1971, may have been a tactical and local affair. Combined with physical attacks in the Belonia region, in November 1971, it must have achieved its aim, as given out by Sukhwant Singh in his *Liberation of Bangladesh,* see end note 3, Chapter IV, on the Battles of Belonia.

18. Headquarters Eastern Command, *Defenders of the Dawn: A Panorama of Eastern Command,* Fort William, Calcutta, 2000, New Delhi, Lancer Publishers and Distributors.

Bangladeshi Authors

Not many books by Bangladeshi authors are available in India. Only three, which I could get hold of and relevant to this study are listed below: The book at serial 4 is about Bangladesh and I cannot confirm the nationality of the author.

1. Azad, Salam, *Contribution of India in the War of Liberation of Bangladesh,* Ankur Prakashani, Dhaka, 2003. The author has given insights to various important decisions, from April 1971, post, the crackdown by the Pakistani Army Units (from West-Pakistan) on the Bengali troops and people, and the beginning of the Freedom Movement, such as:

   (a) In the first week of April, the Government of India took two important decisions. The first was to open the border along Bangladesh, and the second, to allow Bangladesh Government to continue political activities on Indian soil, (p.151).

(b) On April 30, Indian Army was authorised to help the liberation war. On May 9, they started giving training to the Bengali youth (pp.160-163).

(c) In the third week of May, Bangladesh Army was formed.

(d) In May, Indian Government allowed a transmitter, for radio service.

(e) Since July, border conflicts between the Border Security Force (BSF) and Pakistan Army, was a regular phenomenon, and India wanted to get positive results by capturing Border Out-Posts (BOPs) of Pakistan Army. They needed active participation of Bangladesh Sector units in these conflicts.

(f) In August - September, the Bangladesh Government decided to form three battalions named K Force, S Force and Z Force. Their short training was completed in November.

(g) On August 15, naval commando raid by *Mukti Bahini.*

(h) August, September and October, the Pakistani Forces repeatedly shelled Indian Posts in Assam and Tripura. (p.511).

(i) On November 26, Indian troops crossed into Bangladesh, for the second time, in self-defence, in Hilli (p.512).

2. Islam Rafiquil, BU, *A Tale of Millions: Bangladesh Liberation War,;* 1971, Ananna 38/2 Bangla Bazar, Dhaka. First Edition 1974,. Revised Edition 1995.

3. Maniruzzaman Talukder, *The Bangladesh Revolution and its Aftermath,* Bangladesh Books International Limited, Dacca 1980.

4. Observer Research Foundation, New Delhi, Monograph by Yvette Claire Rosser titled *Islamisation of Pakistan: Social Studies Textbooks* (New Delhi: Rupa and Co, 2003) mentions that:

India's military support was omitted from Bangladeshi textbooks after the 1975 assassination of Shiekh Mujibur Rehman. During the seventeen years of military rule, the role of the freedom fighters and their slogan "Joy Bangla" (Long-live Bangladesh) were banned from the textbooks and popular media, replaced by "Bangladesh Zindabad", the Urdu translation. Unlike textbooks published immediately after the war which discussed political and economic exploitation and genocide in erstwhile East-Pakistan, in textbooks published under the military regimes of Bangladesh, who were seeking to normalise relations with their Islamic neighbours, Pakistan is not mentioned, explicitly as the enemy-references are simply to an anonymous enemy army. Many Bangladeshis still harbour resentment against the Pakistani military, but there may be a generation of young adults who are partially unaware that Pakistan was actually 'the enemy', and many mistakenly believe that the Bangladesh army fought the Indian army. When Shiekh Hasina became Prime Minister in 1996, textbooks were again remodified to include the *Mukti judha* (Freedom Fight) and the contributions of her father, Shiekh Mujib (p.68).

I was in for a greater disappointment when, in 2005, on the National Day Bangladesh Government placed a special supplement titled, "Buoyant Bangladesh" in *The Hindustan Times* of New Delhi, on March 30, 2005. It featured special messages from the President and Prime Minister of Bangladesh on the 34th anniversary of independence and National Day. It had no mention of Sheikh Mujib-ur-Rehman, or the role by the Indian Armed Forces, in their liberation of Bangladesh. The ruling coalition of the Bangladesh National Party (BNP) under the leadership of Prime Minister Khaleda Zia (the widow of the military dictator, General Zia-ur-Rahman, who assassinated Mujib), probably has a policy not to acknowledge the contribution of India. It is no surprise that Indo-Bangladesh relations are at the lowest at present. This is a sad case of distorted historiography and it is hoped that truth prevails, irrespective of which political party is in power.

5. Oral history is being underaken by Mr. Mamun-Ur-Rashid of Mukti Juddha Gobeshana Kendra (Freedom Fighters Research Centre, Dhaka).

   Email<mamun-ur-rashid@yahoo.com>

Pakistani Authors and Sources

1. Ali, Tariq, *Can Pakistan Survive ? The Death of a State* Penguin Books, 1983, Chapter 4.
2. Cheema, Parvaiz Iqbal, *The Armed Forces of Pakistan,* Oxford University Press, Karachi, 2002.
3. *Hamoodur Rehman Report: 1971, The Untold Story. The* famous Justice Hamoodur Rehman Commission Report, which was ordered by the Government of Pakistan, was partially declassified in 2001, and one of its version was available openly, in the media. See, 'Moral Lapse, Poor Leadership Caused Pak Debacle in 1971', *Hindustan Times,* New Delhi, January 1, 2001. This Report was accessible on the internet, courtesy Sherlock Holmes, like investigative journalism of the Indian magazine, *India Today, (htpp//www.india-7days.com/ntoday/extra/71war/index.html).* The full version of the report is now available. The Report was the equivalent of the Henderson-Brook Report, ordered by the Indian Government, after our defeat, in the 1962 Sino-Indian War, though it is not yet public. The Hamoodur Rehman Report had recommended a court martial for our opposite divisional commander, Major General M Rahim Khan of 39 (Ad Hoc) Division. The General had managed to escape in a helicopter, just avoiding his capture. The charges against him were:

   (a) Deserting his troops, and areas of responsibility on Chandpur being threatened.
   (b) Willful insistence on day movement, causing death of 18 all ranks, due to staffing by the India Air Force.
   (c) Abandoning communication equipment.
   (d) On December 12, 1971, by word of mouth, causing alarm and despondency.

(e) Avoiding to submit a debriefing, on arrival at the General Headquarters at Pakistan, in 1972.

The Report was also very critical of the performance of Brigadier Mohammad Asla Niazi, the Commander of 53 Infantry Brigade, at Laksham. The Report also recommended a court martial, the charges being:

(a) Showed lack of initiative, determination and planning ability, including preparation of defences at Muzaffarganj (which, on not being prepared, was occupied by the enemy or the Indian Army).

(b) Lack of courage, planning ability and determination to eject enemy at Muzaffarganj, with the result that, contingent of 23 Punjab and elements of 21 AK, surrendered to an Indian unit, on December 11, 1971 in highly adverse circumstances.

(c) Shameful abandoning of Fortress Laksham, on December 9, 1971.

(d) Improper exfiltration of his troops from Fortress Laksham to Comilla, which led to the surrender of 39 Baluch and 400 troops. As a consequence, disintegration of 53 Infantry Brigade.

(e) Abandoning 124 sick and wounded with two medical officers, who were kept deliberately not informed of the exfiltration.

(f) Willfully and intentionally abandoning all heavy equipment and ammunition without a denial plan.

As regards Lieutenant Colonel Yakub Malik, the Commanding Officer of 53 Field Regiment of Pakistan Artillery, the Report mentions that, he ordered in Comilla Cantonment, on the night of March 27/28, 1971, the massacre of Bengali elements of the 40 East Bengal Regiment and other units of Pakistan Army, having Bengali troops.

In its conclusion, the Report brings out three essential conditions for a successful Fortress concept of defence:

(a) Adequate reserves to engage bypassed enemy and give mutual support.

(b) Mutual support between fortresses.

(c) Population not to be hostile.

Lieutenant General AAK Niazi in his book, *The Betrayal of East- Pakistan,* (listed below), was critical of the Hamoodur Rehman Report. He was fully convinced that the leaked extracts were not from the original report. He wondered, why the CO of 25 FF, who lost his nerves and surrendered to the Indian Army, on December 4,1971, went scot free, instead of facing a court martial. The CO, instead was forgiven, as according to General Niazi, he toed the Government line. The October 2000 issue of the Pakistani *Defence Journal* in its Editorial, was critical of the mysterious surfacing of the supplementary report, on the internet, and claimed it to be contradictory in nature, and a Chanakya-like strategy to belittle the Pakistan Army.

At this juncture, when primary sources like official archives in both countries, are not being accessible to scholars, it is unlikely that the complete sequence of events would be known with precision. It is also difficult to comment on the substance and contents of the report. My own assessment is that the Pakistanis lost, due to being out-maneuvered, and then degraded by firepower. At Fortress Laksham, they had no tanks, barely one battery of field artillery, and no air power. On the other hand, we had fire supremacy. As against their 5 to 7 artillery pieces, we had the 23 Artillery brigade of 12 medium guns (27 and 243 Medium batteries), all mountain guns within range (nearly two regiments or 36 guns) and the 18 mortars of 183 Light Regiment (120 mm). This makes it a ratio of about 60 of our artillery guns, against theirs of just six. Or a ratio of 10:1, not counting the infantry mortars.

4. Khan, ZA, Brigadier (Retd.), *The Way it Was,* Ahbas Printers, Karachi, 1998. This is one of the first books that has some details on the battle between the Pakistan Army and the *Mukti Bahini.* The author was the Commanding Officer of 3 Commando Battalion. Belonia was the battlefield of a series of tactical actions between the Bangladeshi forces and Pakistan Army. Before July 1971, two battalions of the Pakistan's 14 Infantry Division, supported by artillery, had failed to dislodge the Bangladeshi forces. Later, two companies of 3 Commando had captured the bulge. The author was posted out from East-Pakistan, to West-Pakistan, before the December War, to raise 38 Cavalry in West-Pakistan. Later, the author was with the 18 Infantry Division, on the western front, against India, in the debacle at Longewala in Rajasthan, in which his ex-unit, the famous 22 Cavalry was involved. Perhaps, this is the first book, which provides a real feel of the planning process of the Pakistani fiasco. It is also by far one the most honest narrative of humans in battle, no different from ours. Unfortunately, the Bombay film industy's *Border,* depicting the Longewala battle, was totally an imaginary affair. Indian cinema needs to do a realistic research on war movies, like the standards of Hollywood war films. The battle study of Longewala, could incorporate this book, as a good reference material. When I was posted at the School of Artillery, in Devlali, in 1998, Major Naser Ahmed from the Bangladesh Army, who was my student mentioned that, in the Staff College in Bangladesh, the battles of Belonia is case study for the students, in the curriculum.

5. Muqueem, Fazal, Major General (Retd.). *Pakistan's Crisis in Leadership.* National Book Foundation, 1973.

6. Niazi, AAK, Lieutenant General, *The Betrayal of EastPakistan,* Manohar Publishers, New Delhi, 1998. The book, by the senior-most Pakistani military commander, as expected, generated a lot of heat and controversy in Pakistan. The author, in the Introduction, refers to Siddiq Salik's, *Witness to Surrender* (listed below), as a pack of lies. He also charges Major General Fazal Muqueem of distortion of facts, in Muqueem's *Crisis in Leadership* (listed below). General Niazi further terms it ironical that, the very General Officer Commanding (Major General Shaukat Riza) of 14 Infantry Division, who was removed by him, was commissioned by the Pakistan Army's General Headquarters (GHQ), to write the official version, as the series on *Pakistan Army* 1966-71 (listed below). Besides his views on the failed leadership of his Commanders, as mentioned above in the paragraph on the *Hamoodur Rehman Report* he had praises for Brigadier MH Atif, the Commander of Mainamati Defences. Niazi records, at page 154, that Commander 117 Brigade, had repeatedly refused the Indian demand for surrender. He made his fortress impregnable and, like his victory, as hockey captain in the 1964 Olympics, he fought hard and was still fighting, when hostilities ended on December 16.

7. Riza, Shaukat, Major General (Retd.).

(a) *Izzat-o-Iqbal,* School of Artillery, published for, and on behalf of, Major General Artillery (MGA), Artillery Directorate, GHQ, Rawalpindi, 1980. This book was not easy to trace in India, till Squadron Leader RTS Chhina (Retd.), of the Centre of Armed Forces Historical Research, at the United Service Institution of India, produced a personal copy for me to refer, in the year 2003. This book begins the war history with India, stating that, on November 21, 1971, Indian troops attacked East-Pakistan. The artillery order of battle of 39 Division, as recorded by him was, 117 Infantry Brigade, with direct support of two batteries (13 Guns); 53 Infantry, with direct support of 5 guns; 91 and 97 Infantry Brigades, each with direct support of a Light Troop of 120 mm mortars. 53 Field Regiment's CO Lieutenant Salim Malik was a Kashmiri. In the operations of 53 Infantry brigade, the author mentions that, on November 20, the brigade was moved to Feni, and occupied positions along the border from Chauddagram-Feni-Belonia. Around November 20, 1971, two guns were deployed, North of Feni, to support 39 Baluch, and three guns were positioned between Feni and Parshuram, to fire around the length and breadth of Belonia salient. The guns in the Belonia salient were commanded by Captain Ahmed-uz-zaman, a Bengali, who did not rebel. According to the author, on November 24, the Indians had infiltrated behind 15 Baluch, and all the five Guns were pulled out of the bulge by November 26, 1971. These dates appear to have been mixed up, as the Belonia Bulge was secured on November 21/22, by 83 and 181 Mountain Brigades, as is given in Chapter IV.

The book also records that, there were nine guns at Laksham. On December 7, 1971, the author records that, 39 Infantry Division got into serious trouble. The Indians had captured Lal Mai, Muzaffarganj and Hajiganj. Command and control was lost. On December 8, 53 Infantry Brigade tried to capture Muzaffarganj. Attempts were a costly failure. On December 9, Eastern Command ordered the brigade to exfiltrate to Comilla. They exfiltrated at 2200 hours on the night of December 9/10. On morning of December 11, remnants of the Brigade trickled into Comilla. Here, 53 and 117 Brigades set up Defences till December 15, 1971.

(b) *The Pakistani Army* 1966-71, Services Book Club, Lahore, Pakistan, 1990. Chapter VI. This book has given the details of Pakistani formations and units.

8. Khan, Saadullah, HJ, Brigadier, *Eastern Pakistan to Bangladesh by an Infantry Brigadier.* Lahore Law Times

Publication, Urdu Bazaar, Lahore. The author was commanding 27 Infantry Brigade of 14 Pakistan Infantry Division, opposite 57 Mountain Division Sector. His spirited account is matched with the tough time he gave to the Indian 57 Mountain Division, in its advance, from Brahmanbaria to Ashuganj, and beyond.

9. Salik, Siddiq, *Witness to Surrender,* Oxford University Press, Karachi, 1977. The author was a prisoner of war for two years after surrender, and has given a very authentic account, from his view point, in Chapter 20. The book includes the unhinging of the Belonia Bulge in November 1971, at page 118. As to the options available for defence, that it is the likely pattern of operations, which could have been adopted by the Pakistani Army, he had given out four options, at page 124. The four options for the defence were:

    I. Defence of the Dacca Bowl.

    II. Deploy on border and gradually withdraw to Dacca Bowl.

    III. Mobile Defence.

    IV. 'Fortress' concept in important border town of Jessore, Jhenida, Bogra, Rangpur, Jamalpur, Maymansingh, Sylhet, Bhairab Bazaar, Comilla and Chittagong.

10. *The Story of the Pakistan Air Force: A Saga of Courage and Honour,* Shaheen Foundation, 1988.

Foreign Authors and Publications, other than from Pakistan and Bangladesh :

1. Carver, Michael, Lord Field Marshal, *War Since 1945*, Weidnerfeld and Nicolson, London, 1980. The author has compared the Indian military operations, to the German blitzkrieg, or the application of Liddell Hart's theory of expanding torrents and indirect approach. This would be a popular reading, as books on and by Liddell Hart are most widely read and quoted by the Indian military.

2. Cloughley, Brain, *A History of the Pakistan Army: Wars and Insurrections,* Oxford University Press, Karachi, 1999.

3. International Institute for Strategic Studies, *Strategic Survey* London : 1971, pp. 46-53.

4. Jackson Robert, *South Asian Crisis India - Pakistan Bangladesh,* Studies in International Security: Published for the International Institute for Strategic Studies (1975).

5. Julian Thomson, Major General, *The Lifeblood of War;* Brassey's (UK), 1991, Chapter 7. *War in a Snipe Marsh: Bangladesh* 1971, pp. 234 - 245.

6. Percival, Spear, *A History of India, Volume Two,* Penguin Books, New Delhi, 1990 pp. 262-263.

7. Sisson Richard and Rose, E, Leo, *War and Secession : Pakistan, India and Creation of Bangladesh,* Vistaar Publications, New Delhi, 1990. This book gives a good account of a series of events and decision which led to the December 1971 War. According to the authors, the war of liberation started with effect from November 21, 1971, when according to them, the Indian Army launched simultaneous military actions on key border regions.

Books and Other Sources on the History of 12 (Poonch) Mountain battery (later redesignated as 27 Poonch Medium battery)

1. Battery History (Manuscript) of 26 Murree and 27 Poonch Batteries.

2. *Outline History of the Regiment of Artillery,* Artillery Institute Press, Deolali.

3. *History of the Indian Artillery,* Indian Army, New Delhi, The Directorate of Artillery, Army Headquarters, 1971.

4. Gaylor, John, *Sons of John Company: The Indian and Pakistani Armies, 1903* - 1991. New Delhi, Lancer International, 1992.

5. Graham CAL, Brigadier, *The History of Indian Mountain Artillery,* Aldershot, Gate and Polden Limited, 1957.

6. MacFetridge CHT and Warron JP' *Tales of the Mountain Gunners,* William Blackwood, Edinburgh 1973, See article "12 (Poonch) Indian Mountain battery, in World War II" by Major AB Howard, the Battery Commander.

7. Rogers, Colonel HCB, *Artillery Through the Ages;* London, Seeley Service & Co, 1971.

8. Trench, Charles Chenevix, *The Indian Army and King's Enemies; 1900* - 1947; London, Thames and Hudson, 1988.

Sources on Jat Sikh and Punjabi Musalman Troops

1. Barstow, Major, AE, *Hand Book of the Indian Army: Sikhs;* Calcutta, Government of India Press, 1928, Revised Edition. The officers of the British Indian Army had written hand books on all the classes and races, that were enrolled. Their work was based on the Gazetteer, personal experiences, field visits and other official sources. These have been written by relatively junior officers and the tone reflects the imperial and colonial mindset. However, the thorough research and data-base, including area study, is a treat to read. No revision has been done till now. Probably, it assumed that, all Indians as citizens, know and have working knowledge of all the diverse castes, classes and communities.

2. Wikeley, Lieutenant Colonel, JM, Seventh Cavalry, Late Recruiting Officer of Punjabi Musalmans, *Hand Book of the Indian Army: Punjabi Musalmans;* Compiled for the Government of India, Revised 1927, Second Edition, 1935.

Sources for Mule Artillery

1. Kapur, Major General, PKD, VSM *Footprints and Milestones: A Story of the Army Service Corps;* Director General, Supply and Transport, Army HQ, 1990.

2. MacFetridge, Charles, *Part III - The Mountain Artillery Mule in the Military Mule; in the British Army and Indian Army: An Anthology;* Privately Published in UK, 2003.

Annexure to Bibliography

(Refer to Official history paragraphs)

Extracts from pages 231 to 235, from the *History of the War in Bangladesh,* which was on the internet, in 2001, by Times of India Group (www.timesofindia.com). covering the operations of IV Corps Zone, in and around the Belonia Bulge, in November 1971

Thus, by the time November was making way to December, the situation in the Indian sub-continent had become unbearably tense. The calculated game of escalation being played by the military regime of Pakistan, which felt assured of foreign help and support, and the failure of the Government of India to secure, through peaceful diplomatic means, a solution to the dangerous problems created by ten million refugees from East-Bengal, had brought the Indian sub-continent to the flash point of a military explosion.

Situation Approaching Undeclared War

With the increasing tempo of *Mukti Bahini* operations and the Pakistan Army's retaliatory actions, the situation all along the Bangladesh border was rapidly deteriorating. Shellings, cross-border raids, ambushes and sabotage became daily occurrences. It became necessary to stop the Pakistan Army's harassment and raids. When the Indian Army units started taking preventive or punitive action, the situation degenerated into almost a state of undeclared war.

Although the Indian Army took charge of the Indo-East Pakistan border in May 1971, for checking ingress of the Pak forces across the international border, it did not involve much in fighting against the Pak troops who entered Indian territory in pursuit of the *Mukti Bahini.* However, it helped the *Mukti Bahini* on many occasions and thus got involved in small skirmishes with the Pak forces of East-Pakistan. As a result, the Pakistani forces started moving very close to and sometimes across the international border, and shelling the Indian border posts. As Pakistani shelling on Indian border villages continued, Eastern Command HQ of the Indian Army permitted Divisional Commanders to take limited offensive actions to eliminate the threat of Pakistani small arms and artillery fire to Indian border villages. However, the Indian Air Force was given strict orders not to fly across the international boundary. But the Pakistan Army continued its provocative activities and raids, and seemed in no way, inclined to de-escalate the mounting tension and violence. So, later it was found necessary even to occupy temporarily certain areas across the border, in order to draw enemy troops closer and to cause maximum casualties to them (221). Four other factors were also responsible for the Army operations, launched in collaboration with the *Mukti Bahini* and the BSF, inside East-Bengal: -

1) To eliminate Pakistani Border Posts or salients from where Pak saboteurs were being continuously launched into the Indian territory to destroy or damage Indian lines of communication and other vital installations.

2) To give the Indian soldiers battle inoculation by 'blooding' them through involvement in actual fighting (222).

3) To improve India's defence posture, so that, in case of bigger operations in future, Indian troops could be on tactically advantageous ground.

4) To ascertain Pak reaction to Indian operations, both at strategic and tactical levels.

Thus, limited trans-border operations were undertaken by the Indian Army at carefully selected places, on all the Formation fronts, along the border. But several of these escalated to fairly deep and large-scale operations, sometimes involving even troops in brigade strength. The operations which require special mention, are detailed below, Corps-wise.

4 Corps Sector

Some small engagements involving the Indian Army had taken place in this Sector earlier, some of which are mentioned below, before taking up the bigger operations of the later period (223).

On 19 June, 7 Raj Rif and 5 Indep. Armd. Sqn. under the control of 61 Mtn Bde (57 Mtn Div), supported by MF, destroyed the Pak BOP at Lati (RH 4624), west of Karimganj, held by elements of 22 Baluch, after inflicting casualties of 11 killed and 2 captured. Some arms and ammunition were also obtained from that place. On August 14, 4 Guard (311 Mtn Bde) exchanged mortar and artillery fire with Pak troops at Alinagar BOP (RR 7635), north of Subhapur, west of river Feni, in which 10 Pak soldiers were killed. On September 28, one coy of *Mukti Fauj* and 2 coys plus one platoon of 18 Rajput, while infiltrating from Bijoynagar to Itakhola-Dharmagarh (RM 5058), east of Brahmanbaria (224), suffered 12 casualties as against about 30 Pak casualties. During October 15-18 , the Mukti Fauj along with elements of 10 Bihar, had an engagement with the Pak forces in the Saldanadi area (north of Comilla) in which the Mukti Fauj suffered 15 casualties, (225) as against the Pak casualties of 16 killed, including *2/Lt* MD Parvez Khan of 33 Baluch.

In another engagement, during October 23-24, one coy of *Mukti Fauj,* 5 platoons of BSF, and elements of 73 Mtn Bde launched an attack against the Pak forces in the Kasba area (north of Comilla) resulting in 35 casualties to the *Mukti Fauj (226).*

Operation in Dhalai (Operation Tomcat)

Dhalai (RN 0385) was a Pak border out-post opposite (some 1,819 metres north of Kamalpur) on the Indian side, in the 61 Mtn Bde Sector (57 Mtn Div under 4 Corps). It had a tea garden and a tea factory where the Pak troops built up a well defended fortress with a platoon of Regulars and EPCAF. It had been subjecting Kamalpur to constant mortar and artillery fire. 1 EB Bn, supported by two coys of 2 Jat, launched an attack on this Pak border post, on the night of October 19/20, but failed to capture it. This was followed by Pak shelling of Kamalpur town on October 21, in which four civilians were killed and 15 others injured. On the night of October 27-28, one EB Regiment succeeded in capturing Patharkhola Tea Estate, but could not occupy Dhalai. Consequently, 2 Jat, supported by 1 Medium battery, 2 Mountain battery, 1 Light battery and two platoons of mortars, crossed the international boundary to launch an attack on Dhalai. Due to stiff Pak resistance, the attack failed to capture the objective (227). On October 30, 1971, 2 Jat launched another attack against the Pak forces, resulting in fierce hand-to-hand fighting. The next day, the Pakistanis brought in some reinforcements, attacked the Jats and held them up. On November 1, 7 Raj Rif from the same Brigade came to the rescue and captured Dhalai after a successful attack. Although the defenders launched several counter-attacks, they were beaten back. The Pakistanis suffered casualties of 70 killed as against the Raj Rif casualties of 7 ORs killed and 4 Officers, including the CO, Lt Col S. Devesan, and 28 ORs wounded (228). Besides 2 Jat's casualties were 44 were killed and 62, including the Brigade Commander, were wounded (229).

With the failure of the initial attacks on Dhalai, its capture perhaps became a prestige issue with the Corps Commander. Hence a more determined attack was launched on the night of October 30/31 under his orders, and allegedly in his presence. It resulted in heavy casualties to both sides, but without any success. Some feel that, "This' had a disturbing effect on all troops .... by putting into doubt the policies and the plans made by officers and interest taken and efforts made, to keep casualties to the minimum"(230). Although an attack by the whole of 61 Mtn Bde ultimately cleared Dhalai on November 3, 1971, the big effort and the total casualties of 51 killed and 94 wounded suffered by the Indian Brigade, were hardly justified by the result. Its contribution, however, was certainly valuable in blooding the 'raw' Indian troops, facing 'seasoned' Pak soldiers, with seven months of operational experience in East-Bengal.

Operations in Belonia Bulge

83 Mtn Bde Group of 23 Mtn Div had concentrated for operation 'Cactus Lily', in Belonia Sector by 4 October and took over operational responsibility in area Belonia RR 629677, Srinagar and Samarganj from 73 Mtn Bde by 17 October. The Belonia Bulge, approximately 8 km by 11 km jetting northward from Fenny into Tripura, was under the occupation of seven platoons of 15 Baluch, 11 platoons of EPCAF and 70 Razakars. 23 Mtn Div employed 83 Mtn Bde (2 Rajput and 3 Dogra), supported by 57 Mtn Regt, battery 24 Med Regt, battery 183 Lt Regt, eight coys of *Mukti Fauj* and 300 Freedom Fighters in order to straighten the line of control and clear the Pak forces from the area. After infiltration into the enemy-held territory during November 5/6, 1971, (231) the Indian Forces attacked Parashuram .(RR 6364) at 2030 hrs on 8 November. After some fighting Parashuram was captured the next day. 3 Dogra suffered minor casualties, as against Pak casualties of 28 killed, and 55 wounded or taken prisoner (232). Meanwhile, on November 8, two platoons of 2 Rajput and two BSF platoons captured Belonia Railway Station (RR 6267) after a good fight, in which 2 Rajput suffered minor casualties as against heavy casualties inflicted on the adversary. Soon afterwards, four Pak Sabre jets strafed Indian troops on November 9, when one of them was damaged by MMG fire from 3 Dogra (233). Next day, four Sabres came again and strafed Indian positions, but three of them were damaged by Indian Air Defence guns. Having thus cleared the Pak forces from the northern part of the Belonia Bulge through 'Operation Winter Frost', action was taken to free other parts of the bulge from Pakistani hands. This necessitated the strengthening of 83 Mtn Bde by bringing 14 Kumaon under its command.

Under 'Operation Skylark', it was planned to capture Phulgazi (RR 6055) as the first step for ridding the southern part of the Belonia Bulge of the Pakistanis (234). On November 16, 'A' Coy of 14 Kumaon launched an attack against the Pak force, in

Phulgazi area, but could not make much headway due to Pak shelling, MMG and small arms fire. However, this Coy captured the central part of the area after heavy fighting from bunker to bunker. Subsequently, both 'A' and 'B' Coys' beat back two enemy counter-attacks, but in view of stiff Pak resistance and continuous artillery fire, 14 Kumaon was withdrawn from the objective and concentrated at Gabtala (RR 5654). In this action, the Indian troops suffered casualties of one Officer and 10 ORs killed, one Officer, 1 JCO and 31 ORs wounded (235).

Due to the failure of this operation, a new operation 'Operation Harvest' - was launched for capturing the whole of Belonia Bulge, up to the lateral road Gangadhar Bazar (RR 7142) - Birinchi (RR 5841). 181 Mtn Bde and the Kilo Force were added to 83 Mtn Bde for this purpose. The Pakistanis also built up their strength, comprising 15 Baluch, 39 Baluch, one Battalion EPCAF, 3 to 4 Light Tanks, (236) one Field battery and one section of heavy mortars, spread over Ramgarh (RR 9337), Subhapur (RR 7333), Chhagalnaiya (RR 3842), Feni (RR 5758) and Jagannath Dighi (RR 4853)(237). According to plan, on the night of 22/23 November, 83 Mtn Bde and 181 Mtn Bde moved from the west and the east respectively after road blocks were established against the Pak movement, in their respective areas. By the first light of November 23, all movements of Pak forces along both road access, were effectively blocked, except for a gap of about 1,830 metres between the two Brigades which held strong Pak positions at Munshirhat (RR 6050). Unfortunately, during the night, the Pakistanis pulled out with their guns and equipment through this gap, leaving behind a few pockets to simulate activity. The same day, various Units were engaged in clearing the Pak pockets, and one armd sqn, alongwith 'D' Coy 9 Kumaon, tried to cross Muhari river, which was a big tank obstacle. After much reconnaissance, the river could be crossed at 0600 hours the next day and the Indian troops captured Phulgazi, by 1200 hours. On November 25, 14 Kumaon fought bloody engagements at Mridhyar Bazar (RR 6845) which caused considerable casualties to both sides (238). Consequently, one armd sqn was sent in an out-flanking move from the south which unnerved the Pak force. With the dislodgement of the

Pak force from Mridhyar Bazar, the whole of Belonia Bulge was secured, and on November 30, operational control of Belonia Bulge was handed over to the Kilo Force. Pak casualties in Operation Harvest were about 50 killed and 13 taken Prisoners of War, as against one Officer, one JCO and 6 ORs of 14 Kumaon killed and one wounded. The result of this operation was somewhat unsatisfactory, as the Pakistanis pulled out after the initial battle.

It should be noted that, the Border Roads Organisation had improved and constructed roads from Agartala, into and around the Belonia Bulge, which could sustain subsequent operations, undertaken in this sector after D-Day.

References (Extracts)

221.	From official records
222.	Ibid
223.	Main 4 Corps HQ came to this area in September 1971
224.	The Pakistan casualty figures should be taken only as estimates, from official records
225.	From official records
226.	From official records
227.	From official records
228.	From official records
229.	The whole of 61 Mountain Brigade had to be launched to clear the enemy from the post which was captured on November 3. From official records
230.	Sodhi, Brig. HS, *Operation Windfall, Emergence of Bangladesh,* pp.142-143
231 to 238	From official records.

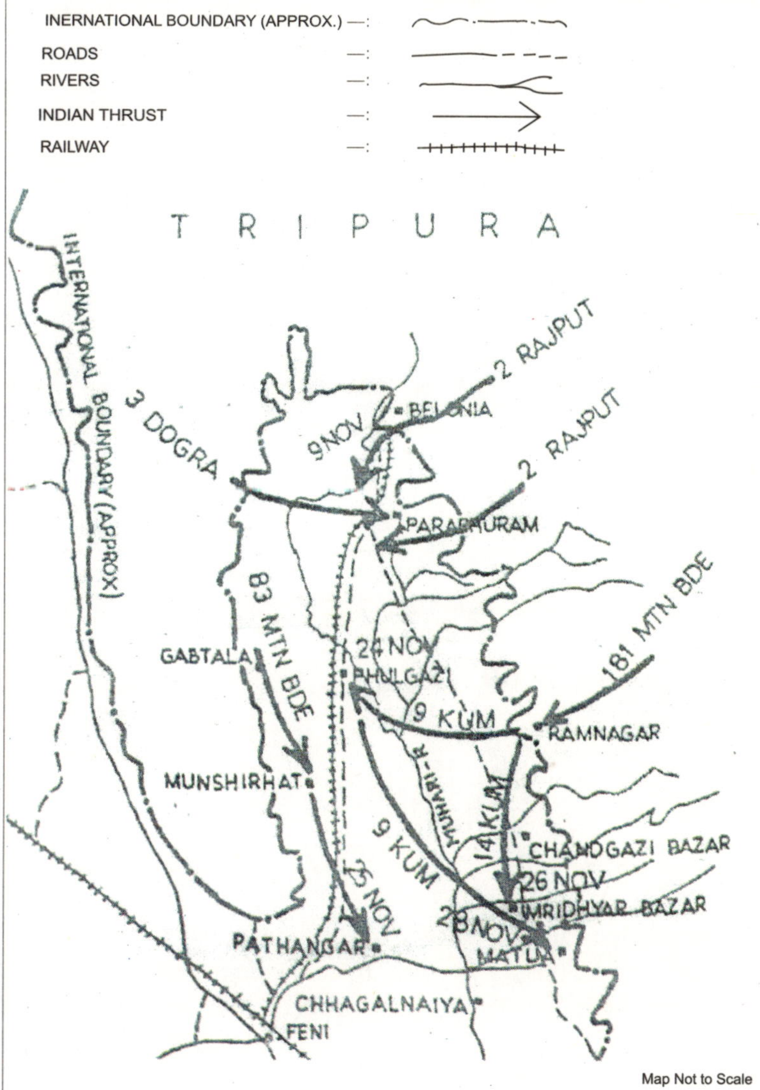

Sketch Map of Belonia Bulge

Index

1 Armoured Squadron, 64, 69, 70, 73, 77, 82
2 Jat, 174
2nd Kohat Mountain Battery, 88
2 Rajput, 79, 81, 152
3 Dogra, 51-53, 65, 156, 157
  Capture ofParshuram by- 53
3 Kumaon (Rifles), 73
4th Lahore Battery, 88
5 Mountain Division, 15
5 Mountain Division Sector, 78
5 Mountain Regiment, 95
6 Jat, 61, 63, 64
7 Armoured Brigade, 98
7 Indian Division, 81
7 Kumaon, 83
7 Rajput (Rifle), 83
8 Mountain Division, 70, 95
8 Mountain Division Sector, 76
9 (Native) Mountain Battery, 91
9 Mountain Battery, 87
10 Bihar, 42, 58
10 Field Regiment, 21
12 (Poonch) Mountain Baty, 88, 97, 99, 100, 102, 106-109
12 Kumaon, 157
14 Garhwal Rifle, 78
14 Infantry Division, 33, 51
14 Jat., 79
14 Kumaon, 55, 62, 63, 64, 176
14 Pakistan Infantry Division, 167
15 Baluch, 85
17 Infantry Brigade, 34
20 Mountain Division, 152
21 Azad Kashmir, 51, 76
21 Intl. Light Mountain Battery, 88
23 Artillery Brigade, 71
23 Mountain Division, 43, 46, 51, 70, 75, 76, 77
23 Mountain Regiment, 23, 32, 34
23 Punjab, 76, 81, 86
23 Punjab (Pak), 75
24 Medium Regiment, 15, 16, 84, 87, 95, 143, 144
25 Frontier Force Baty (Pak), 73
25 Frontier Forces, 76
26 Indian Infantry Regiment, 104
26 Medium Battery, 70
26 Murree Medium Baty, 31, 32, 94
27 (Poonch) Medium Baty, 18, 24, 34, 37, 98, 107, 156
27 Medium Baty, 56, 58, 75, 77, 84

28 Medium Baty, 32
29 Mountain Baty, 91
29 Pakistan Baty, 91
39 Baluch, 57, 76, 85
39 Infantry Brigade, 33
39 Infantry Division, 51, 76, 102
48 Air Defence Regiment, 54, 57
53 Field Regiment, 166
53 Infantry Brigade, 162, 166
57 Mountain Baty, 70
57 Mountain Division, 31, 32, 46, 70, 82
57 Mountain Regiment, 51-56, 70
61 Mountain Brigade, 70, 79, 83
82 Light Regiment, 22
83 Mountain Brigade, 51-53, 57, 69, 70, 75, 81, 82, 83
97 Infantry Brigade, 35
101 Communication Zone, 82
109 Murree Battery, 91
124 Divisional Locating Baty, 42, 82
181 Mountain Brigade, 55, 57, 63, 71, 75, 79, 166
18l/61 Mountain Brigade, 82, 84
183 Light Regiment, 22, 77, 79
197 Mountain Regiment, 70, 83
198 Mountain Regiment, 58, 71
202 Infantry Brigade, 33
243 Medium Baty, 32, 37, 42, 43, 46, 70, 77, 83, 89, 95
301 Mountain Brigade, 70, 73, 75, 77, 79, 81-83, 86, 156
313 Infantry Brigade, 33

AAK Niazi, 34, 163, 165
Aatgram and Chargram, 37
Abbotabad, 87,90,91
Abdul Khaliq, Sub, Pak Champion, 143
Acoustics Means, 62
Admin Box, 103, 104, 106, 108
Agartala, 31, 38, 40, 43, 85, 177
Agartala Airport, 40
Air Observation Aircraft (Bird Dog), 54
Air Observation Post, 53; 56, 77, 84
Air Traffic Control Tower, Agartala, 40
Akhaura, Border Town, 40, 41
Akhaura-Brahmanbaria, 51
Alex, Gen., 115
Amar Post, 78
American Mission School, 112
Arakans, 102, 104,117
Army
  Education Corps (AEC), 16
  Rule, 27
  Service Corps, 77, 78
  Service Corps Convoy, 17
Artillery
  Association, 24
  Centre, Nasik, 69
  Intelligence, 41
Arunachal Pradesh, 11,95
Aslam Niazi, Brig., 51
Assam, 19,20,31
Athlye, Maj., 16
Aurora, Jagjit Singh, Lt. Gen., 36
Avtar Singh, Maj., 52, 56
Awami League, 27
Ayub Khan, FM, 27

Badarpur, 22, 23,38
Bagshawe, Lt., 104, 108
Bajaj, SC, 33
Balbir Singh, Naib.Sub., Champion, 19, 20, 25, 88, 143
Baldev Singh, Naib Sub., 129

Baluch Battalions, 51
Banerjee, Ashish, Lt.Col., 32, 42, 71, 84
Bangladesh, 95, 11, 146, 153, 158, 159
  Army, 159, 160, 164
  Border, 164, 171
  Creation of-, 28, 145
  Liberation of-,12, 29, 160
  Liberation War, 35
  National Party (BNP), 160
  War, 11
  War 1971, 146
Battle Locations, 11
Battle of
  Admin Box, 81,98, 102, 103
  Akhnoor-Chamb, 107
  Arakan, 106
  Belonia, 46, 146, 158, 164
  Belonia Bulge, 49
  Kohima, 106
  Ngakyedauk Pass, 103
  Zakiganj, 76
Bay of Bengal, 31,49
Bayek, 42
Belonia, 34, 49, 51, 52, 53, 55, 69, 85, 144, 152, 158, 164
  Bulge, 34, 49, 51, 55, 58,166, 167, 175, 177
  Operation, 51,64
Bengal Sappers, 155
Bengal Troops, 158, 162
Bengali
  Freedom Movement, 148
  Insurgency, 28
Bengalis,, 27, 28
Bhairab Bazar, 33
Bhanwar Singh, 2Lt., 157
Bhuttar, SS, Maj., 57, 61
Bidwell, Shelford, Maj. Gen., 98, 102
Bihar, West Bengal and Assam, 17
Bishenpur, 117
Bofors, 116
Bofor Guns, 56
Bombay Native Artillery, 90
Bomdila, 18
Border Outpost, 53, 159
Border Outpost of-, 51
  Belonia, 51
  Parshuram, 51, 53
Border Road Organization (BRO), 177
Border Security Force (BSF), 31, 159, 172, 175
Border Towns of-, 167
  Bhairab Bazaar, 167
  Bogra, 167
  Comilla and Chittagong, 167
  Jamelpur, 167
  Jessore, 167
  Jhenida, 167
  Mymansingh, 167
  Rangpur, 167
  Sylhet, 167
Bourke, Brig., 113
Brahamanbaria, 173
Brahmanbaria City, 40
Brahmanbaria to Ashuganj, 167
Brar, Rupinder Singh, Cap., 79, 85
British
  Army, 98
  Navy, 66
  Pattern, 61
Burma, 15, 16, 33, 51, 88, 89, 91, 98, 101, 102, 106
  Campaigns, 24, 100, 106, 107, 111, 112
  Liberation of-, 88

Buschi (Left of Comilla), 47, 75-78, 144, 155
Buschi Forest, 77

Cannichael, 117
Ceasefire, 47, 84, 85
Centre of Armed Forces Hist. Research, (CAFHR), 146
Chandgi Bazaar, 64
Chandpur, 51, 55, 70, 79, 81-83, 85, 86, 161
  Axis, 76
  Committee Areas, 84
  Port, 34
Chaudagram, 34
Chagalnaiya, 176
Chaudagram-Feni-Belonia, 166
Chaudagram Defence, 75
Chaudagram-Parikot-Laksham Axis, 70
Chawla, CD, Cap, 33
Chhina, RTS, Squadron Leader, 165
Chindwin Valley, 101
Chinese, 18, 19,28, 119, 150
Chinese Attack, 153
Chinese Sector of Sela, (NEFA), 70
Chittagong, 82, 83
Chittagong Hill Tract, 35
Chopra, AS, Maj. Gen., 156
Clement Town (Dehradun), 21
College of Military Engineering Poona, 64
Comilla, 34, 51, 82, 84,107,166
Comilla and Maynamati, 31,46
Comilla and Maynamati Cantonments, 82
Comilla Cantonment, 162
Comilla to Chaudagram, 51
Comilla-Maynamati Complex, 69
Corps Maintenance Area (CMA), 31
Counter Bombardment, 58, 62, 69, 84
  Organization, 71
Court Marshall, 162
Cowan, Punch, 114

Dacca, 28,33,78,79,82,83, 146, 151
Dacca Bowl, 167
Dahung, 17, 18, 19
Daudkandi, 51
Danish Ships, 66
Darshan Singh, Naik, 23, 134
Das, OK, 2Lt., 157
Daukhandi, 34, 83
December 1971 General War, 73
Defensive Fire Tasks, 41
Dehra Dun, 21
Desert Army, 117
Devesan, S, Col, 174
Dhalai, 174
Dhampur, 46,69
Dharmanagar, 31
Dim Dam fly, 17
Dirang, 18
Division Maintenance Centre, 103, 104
Diwan, Satish Chand, (OPO), 32
Dogra Regiment Centre, 65, 156
Drive Mule Battery, (DMA), 91
Dual Meet (Indo-Pak Sports Fixture), 143

East Africa, 88
East India Company, 90
East Pakistan, 11,22,27-29,38,41, 75,95, 148, 160,164, 165
  Borders, 18
  Civil Armed Police (EPCAP), 57
  Eastern Border, 11

Egypt and Palestine, 88
Electronic
Deception Plan, 158
Media, 14
Warfare, 84
Elsworth, Nigel, Maj., 111, 112, 121
Flton, Miles, 113
Extreme Cold Climate (ECC), 18

Fakir Singh, Sr.JCO, 18, 54, 57, 79, 132
Falkland Campaign, 36
Fateh Singh, Sub., 88
Feni, 55, 57, 140, 166, 176
Feni HQs., 34
Feni and Belonia, 51
Feni and Parshuram, 166
Feni Chittagong Road, 34
Feni-Fulgazi-Belonia Meter Gauge Rly Stn., 52
Fire Plan (Dam Busters), 53
Fire Plan (Fire Correct), 56
Fire Plan (Garam Masala), 42
First World War, 88
Fortress Laksham, 162, 163
Forward
Line of Defence, 54, 57
Observation Officer, (FOO), 53, 55,94,106
Freedom
Fighters, 29, 160, 175
Movement, 158
Movement in Bangladesh, 28
Frontier Force Battery, 91
Fulgazi, 55, 57, 63

Gandhi, Mrs. Indira, 152
Gangadhar Bazar, 176
Garrison Hockey Field, 21
Garuband, 43, 52
Gautam, PK, Col., 12
Gazaria, 40, 41-43,58
Gazaria Observation Post, 158
General Elections, 27
German Thrust through Ardeness, 31
Graham, CAL, Brig., Gen., 24, 98, 104, 108
Great War of Independence (1857), 90
Guerilla Operation, 29
Gun Position Officer (GPO), 24, 25, 37, 38, 46, 58, 63, 69, 139
Gunnery, 15
Gunnery Problems, 139
Gupta, VK, 2Lt, (GPO), 32,46,70
Gurbax Singh, Haval (Sena Medal), 77
Gurbhej Singh, Gunner, 43
Gurcharan Singh, Hav, 83,133,143

Hajiganj, 79, 85,166
Hamoodur Rehman Commission Report, 144, 161,163,165
Harbhajan Singh, Maj., 58, 135
Hardip Singh, Naib Sub, 18, 46, 63, 66, 70, 132
Hazara, 90, 91
Henderson-Brook Report, 161
Hira, RD, Maj Gen., 77,135
History of 1962, 1965, 1971 Wars, 146
Horse Artillery, 94
Hoshiar Singh, Brig., 33
Howard, AB, Maj, 25
Howitzers, 89, 9 1,98, 107
Human Rights Atrocities, 144
Hume, John George Learmouth, 111, 112, 114

Imphal (Manipur), 98,101, 116,121
Imphal-Kohima Area, 102
India and Pakistan, 28
Indian
  Air Force, 29, 35, 161, 172
  Armed Forces, 29, 160
  Army, 14,23,29,34,78,81,147, 151,159,163,171-173
  Artillery, 78, 88
  Infantry Battalion, 58
  Military, 28
    Academy (IMA), 15,40
    History, 97
    Leadership, 152
  Mountain Artillery, 90
  Posts, 159
Indo-Bangladesh Relations, 160
Indo-East Pakistan Border, 172
Indo-Gangetic Plains, 27
Indo-Pakistan
  Encounter, 13
  War, 145
  War 1965, 24, 89, 94, 95, 107, 146, 150
  War 1971, 95, 152
  War (1965/1971), 149
Infantry Units, 64
Infiltration, 73, 103
Information
  and Cyber War, 13
  Technology Age, 94
Institute for Defence Studies and Analyses, (IDSA), 153
International
  Boundary, 40
  Community, 153
Iqbal Singh, Lt., MC, 88, 94
Ist Burma Corps, 98
Ist Indian Field Brigade, 90
Jacob, JFR, Lt.Gen., 78
Jadhav, S, Maj., 32, 37, 38, 70
Jagannath Dighi, 176
Jagati, BCS, Cap, 19, 32, 62, 84
Jagatpur Post, 64
Jagdev Singh, Brig., 65, 66, 152
Jagdish Singh, Hav, 133
Jammu and Kashmir, 28, 146, 153
Janson, John, Lt., 99, 113-117
Japanese, 88, 102, 103, 104
  Attack of Burma, 98
  In Burma, 81
Japs, 113-116 *see* Japanese also
Jat Regiment, 57
Jat Sikhs, 15, 18, 91
Jat Sikh Operators, 84
Jat Troops, 58
Jatiapur, 33
Jawala Singh, Sub., 114-116, 118
Jit Singh, Hav., 133
Jit Singh, Naib Sub, 143
Jodha, JS, Lt., 33, 38, 40, 81
Joginder Singh, Hav, 133
John, Pegu, 118, 119

Kabal Singh, Hav, 56, 133
Kailashahar Area, 47
Kakraban (Tripura), 83, 143
Kala, HB, Maj., 57
Kalewa Crossing, 116
Kalha, SS, 89
Kalia, VK, Cap, 55
Kalikrishnagar (KK Nagar), 69
Kalikrishnagar-Buschi Axis, 71
Kamalpur, 173, 174
Kanglatonbi Camp, 117, 121
Kargil, 13
Karimganj, 173
Karimganj and Kailashahar, 70

Kartar Singh, 2Lt, 32, 88, 104, 108
Kehar Singh, Hav, 55, 84, 133
Khalid Musharraf, Mukti Bahini, Maj., 58
Khan, ZA, Brig., 164
Kheela Singh, 134
Khopkar, CP, Maj., 19, 37, 131
Khuller, SD, Lt.Col., 71
Khurana, SD, Lt. Col., 77
Kilo Force, 31,83
Kipling Pagoda, 112, 116
Kitkule, PD, Maj.(Vir Chakra), 22
Kohima, 88
Kohima Garrison, 106
Kraz Field Artillery Tractor, 19
Kumaon Hills, 17

Lachman Singh, Maj. Gen., 85,152
Laksham, 34, 49, 55, 70, 75, 77-79, 81, 82, 86, 144, 162, 166
  and Buschi, 85
  Defences, 76
  Fall of-, 82
  to Comilla, 162
  to Feni, 65
Lalmai, 85
  Defence, 70
  Hills, 75, 79
  Rly Station, 82
Lalmuki, 51
Lasrado, GM, Maj., 32
Latu Rly Station, 38
Latu to Tits River, 33
Lentaigne, Joe, 114
Liberation of Goa, 146
Lightning Campaign, 150
Line of Control, 64
Longewala (Rajasthan), 164
Loomba, Iqbal Singh, GPO, 76
Lumding Station, 22
Lunt, Jimmy, 118

Major Singh, 134
Malaria, 17
Malkit Singh, 134
Manekshaw, SHFJ, COAS, 28, 29, 35, 151
Mannu Bazar, 46
Maritime Training, 147
Masba, 43
Master Plan (March to Delhi), 102
Maynamati, 83, 84
  Ceremony, 12
  Complex, 70, 82
Maynamati and Laksham, 76
McCiag, R, Col. MC, 24, 89, 108, 110, 112
Media Wars, 14
Medium Forward Observation Officer, 61,62
Medium Observation Post Officer, 58
Meghalaya, 19, 31
Mellors, JP, 110
Meter Gauge Rly Station, 22
Mian Bazar, 34, 51, 73, 75, 76
Mian Mir, 91
Mike Party, 54, 156
Military
  Leadership India, 149
  Medal, 104, 105, 108
  Operation, 150
Ministry of Defence Hist. Division, 146
Misamari, 19, 22
  Transit Camp, 17
Mohammad Asla Niazi, Brig., 162
Mohammad Rahim Khan, Maj. Gen. Court Marshall, 161

Mohinder Singh, Hav, 20, 23, 51, 52, 81, 133
Moulmein, (Burma), 98, 112, 113, 117, 118, 120
Mountbatten, Lord, 105
Mridhyar Bazaar, 176, 177
Mudaffarganj-Hajiganj-Chandpur Axis, 75
Muhajirs/Refugees, 27
Mujibur Rahman, 27, 28, 160
Mukti Bahini (MB), 29, 31, 42, 53, 55, 58, 81, 84, 135, 136, 147, 149, 154, 159, 164, 172
  Ferocious Guerilla Fight, 136
  Forces, 81,148
  Naval Guerrillas, 154
  Operation, 171
  Operations, 42
  Scouts, 61
  Targets, 41
Mukti Fauj, 29, 37, 38, 173, 175
Mukti Judha, 160
Mukund Singh, Hav., 104, 105, 108
Mule Artillery, 89, 169
Munshirhat, 176
Murree Battery, 90-95
  Animal and Equipment of-, 91
  Background of-, 90
  Guns Used By-, 92
  Post-Independence Operations, 94-95
Murree Mountain Battery, 91
Muslim Dominated Areas, 27
Muslims and Hindus, 27
Muzaffarganj, 77, 162, 166

Nachattar Singh, Lance Naik, 134
Nandanagar, 40
Narang Singh Gunner, 43
Naser Ahmad, Maj, 164
National Assembly, 28
National Day Bangladesh, 160
Natural Resources, 27
Navneet, Swaraj, 2Lt, 16
Nelson, Hortio, 66
Ngakyedauk Pass, 103-106
Niazi, Gen., 34,163,165
Nilaki Area, 55
Nirbhayapur-Bhagmara-Buschi Axis, 71
North Bihar, 4]
North East Frontier Agency (Now Arunachal Pradesh), (NEFA) 15, 17, 18, 20, 22, 31, 37, 38, 88, 95
North East of India, 31
North Tripura, 31
North West Frontier, 90
North West Frontier Provinces, 79
Northern Glaciers, 78

Observation Posts, 40, 41, 42
  Agartala, 40
  Gazaria, 40
Observation Post Officer, 51, 53, 55-57, 73, 79, 83
  Parties, 51, 58, 69
Open Action Hajiganj, 156
Operation
  Arakans, 88
  Belonia, 139
  Cactus Lily, 177
  Counter Insurgency, 3 I
  Goa, 151
  Harvest, 57, 177
  In Belonia Bulge, 175
  In Dhalai, 173
  Nepal, 89, 107
  Parakram, 150

Skylark, 175
Sultana, 55
Tomcat, 173
Vijay (Goa), 89
Windfall, 153
Winter Frost, 175

Pakistan, 27, 28, 33, 51, 89, 148, 150, 160, 161, 171
53 Brigade, 55
39 Division, 76
117 Brigade, 75
Air Force, 35, 167
Army, 41, 57, 81, 82, 84, 136, 143, 158, 159, 162-164, 171
Army (POW), 143
Army Deployment, 33
Army in East Pakistan, 29
Artillery, 41, 56, 76, 84, 144, 157
Attack on India, 42
Attack on Kutch, 153
Border, 37, 173
Border Observation Post at Lati, 173
Border Posts, 172, 173
Defence, 64
Defenders, 78
Forces, 41, 63, 69
Deployment of-, 51
Forces of East Pakistan, 172
Gunners, 41, 42, 77
Intruders, 84
Interdivisional Boundary with-, 51
Infantry, 107
Military, 160
Military Leadership, 153
Observation Post, 85, 155
People's Party (PPP), 28
Radio Operators, 84
Sabre Jets, 54, 175
Snipers, 41
Troops, 12, 63, 75, 82, 136, 172, 174
Palit, DK, Maj. Gen., 150, 153
Palsukar, RD, Col, VC,65,67, 156
Pargat Singh (BHM), 133
Parshuram, 53, 55, 57
Partition of 1947, 79
Partition of India and Pakistan, 27
Parvez Khan, 2Lt., 173
Pathans, 27
Patharkhola Tea Estate, 174
Paul, Capt., National and Service Squash Champion, 16
Pedgaonkar, AR, Cap, 19,46,51-53, 55,56,131
Pegu, 114
Peshawar Mountain Battery, 90
Phillora, 107
Phulgazi, 175, 176
Pir Baksh Hat, 63
Planners, 28
Portuguese, 89
Praval, KC, 66
Presidency Armies of Bengal, Madras and Bombay, 90
Price, RJ Lloyd, Maj, 118
Prismatic Campus, 21
Prisoners of War (POWs), 81,149, 177
Prome, 115
Promodnagar Area, 38
Punjab, 91
Frontier Campaigns, 91
Irregular Force Battery, 90
Punjabi Musalmans (PMs), 88, 91, 98,99
Foreign Tribes, 88

Gujjars, 88
Jats, 88
Rajputs, 88
Troops, 169
Punjabis, 27

Qazi Abdul Majeed, Maj. Gen., 33
Quadrant Elevation (QE), 140

Rahim Khan, Maj., 33
Raids on-, 147
Chalna,147
Chittagong, 147
Khulna, 147
Mangla, 147
Rajendra Nath, Maj.Gen., 149
Ramanand, Baty Commander, Maj., MC, 35, 37, 46, 55, 57, 63, 69, 73, 131
Ramgarh, 176
Ran Singh, Sub., 70, 77
Rangoon, 118
Ranjit Singh, 134
Rankina, 120
Rathee, RS, 33
Rautela, PS, Cap, 57
Razakars, 175
Razmak, 79, 114
Reconnaissance Parties, 76, 79, 81
Regimental Command Post, 62
Rivers, 98
Brahmputra, 28, 121
Chindwin, 98
Fena, 35
Ganga, 28
Gumti, 43, 51
Irrawady, 98
Meghna, 28, 31, 33, 34, 51, 79, 82
Padma, 28
Salveen, 98
Sittang, 98
Riza, Shaukat, Maj. Gen., 165
Rocket Launchers, 78
Romell, Erwin, German FM, 22, 151
Royal Artillery, 90
Rubber Plantations, 112
Russia, 16
Sadullah Khan, Brig., 33
Sagat Singh, Lt. Gen., 36, 149, 151, 152
Saldanadi, 33, 34, 42, 51
Saleemullah, Brig., 33
Salim Malik, Lt.,Col., 166
Salvation, 119
Sandhu, Gurcharan Singh, Maj. Gen., 151
Sandhu RS, Cap, 69,83, 132
Sangars, 79
Sapper Camps, 18
Sappers, 11
Sarbans Singh, Maj., 152
Sarin, Raj, 2Lt., 157
Satnam Singh Opal, 135
School of Artillery, Devalali (Maharashtra), 15, 16,23,25,41, 65 129 164
Second Afghan War, 91
Second Sikh War, 90
Second World War, 15, 16, 24, 31, 61, 81, 87, 88, 108, 111
Sector,
Ashuganj, 31
Akhaura Brahmanbaria, 31
Belonia, 53
Comilla, 53
Eastern, 31
Sela, 12, 18, 19, 95
Sialkot, 94, 70, 89, 95, 107

Sela, 12, 15, 18, 19, 95
Sela and Bomdila, 15
Sela Defence, 12
Sena Medal, 77
Sessa, 17
Shaktiman Trucks, 17
Shaktiman Vehicles, 95
Shamsherpur Tea Gardens, 47
Sharma, Bhartendu, Cap., 78
Sharma, DL (QM), 33
Sharma, KC, Cap, 33, 42, 71
Sheikh Hasina, 160
Sheikh Mansoor Hussain Atif, Brig., 34, 51, 84, 85, 144, 165
  Commander of Pakistani Forces, 107
Sheikh Mujibur Rahman, 27, 28, 160
  Assassination, 160
Sher Singh, 58
Shillong, 22
Shoopur, 33
Shwegyin, 115-117
Siachen Glacier, 78
Sialkot, 89, 107
Sihota, Maj., 53
Sikh Troops, 61, 77, 136
Sikkim, 151
Silchar, 23
Sindhis, 27
Sino-Indian Border, 95
Sino-Indian War 1962, 33, 146, 150, 161
Sinzewya Box, 103, 106
Sittang, 113
Sittang Bridge Disaster, 99
Sittang Brigade, 88
Six Point Proposal, 28
Slim, Lt. Gen., FM, 98, 101-103
Smyth, Gen., 114
Society, Pluralist, 27
Sonamura, 43, 51
Sondhi, GS, Brig, 152
Sr.Observation Post Officer, 69
Struggle for Freedom (East Pakistan), 28
Subhapur, 176
Subrahmanyam, K, 153
Subramaniyam, RI, Maj., 58
Suhil/Shadam Singh, Sub, (OBI), 94
Sukhwant Singh, Maj. Gen., 63, 65, 66, 152, 158
Sumer Singh, Sub.Maj., 77
Sunamganj, 33
Suppression of the Mutiny, 144
Surender Singh, 58
Sylhet, 31, 33, 51
Sylhet District, 38

Tactical Plan, 70
Talwar, SK, Col., 15, 25
Tango Battery, 46
Tashkent Agreement (1960),89
Taskeen-ud-din, Brig, 34
Taukhyamstan, 119
Technical Characteristics of Ordnance, 123 -126
Tenga Valley, 11
Thaman Singh, 32
Tiddim, 117
Tiwari, Havaldar, Weapon Instructor, 41
Training Camps, 147
Trans Border Guerrilla Raid on Lathitilla, 147
Transport and Communication, 29
Tributaries, 29
Tripura, 19, 31, 38, 49, 175
Tripura and Mizo Hills, 31

Troop Games, 17
Tropic of Cancer, 85
Two Nation Theory, 27
United
  Nations, 153
  Service Institution of India, 146
  States Information Institute, 165
US Army Design, 62
Uttar Pradesh, 27

Vishramganj, 46

Wagon Lines, 77
War of Independence, 90
War with Pakistan, 153
Warfare, 13, 94
Wariam Singh, Sub., 22
Watchman, G de V, Brig., 118
West Pakistan, 27, 28
Wilberforce, Hugh, 112
Wolfe, RC, Cap., 42, 51, 52, 57, 69, 75
Wolfe, RC., Maj., 132
Woods, Sammy, Brig., 120
World War II, 15, 16, 24, 31, 61, 81, 87, 88, 108, 111
Worthington, Cap, 105

Yahya Khan, Gen., 27, 28
Yakub Malik, Lt.Col., 162
Yogananda, Paramhansa, 65
Yom Kippur War, 36

Zakiganj, 46
Zakiganj Capture, 70
Zia-ur-Rahman, Gen., 160